D0115078

PENGUIN 1

Heaven

Jacky Newcomb is known the world over as 'The Angel Lady'. She is a multi-award winning, *Sunday Times* bestselling author and regular columnist for *Take a Break's Fate & Fortune* magazine. Jacky has published literally hundreds of articles, including real-life experiences of angels, afterlife, life between lives and life after death. She has been studying the phenomena of paranormal experiences for thirty-five years and is one of the UK's leading experts.

She regularly appears in the national press (*Daily Mirror, Daily Mail, Daily Express*) and is frequently featured in magazines such as *Real, Chat, Woman, Bella, Woman & Home, Spirit & Destiny*, and many others.

Jacky often appears on radio as a paranormal experiences expert and her expertise is also sought for television programmes such as ITV's *This Morning* and Channel 5's *Live with Gabby Logan*.

Jacky gives talks and runs workshops all over the country. She has worked with many famous names and has several celebrity clients.

For more information about Jacky and her work visit www.JackyNewcomb.com and follow her on Facebook and Twitter.

Heaven

Incredible true stories of the afterlife

JACKY NEWCOMB

PENGUIN BOOKS

PENGUIN BOOKS

Published by the Penguin Group
Penguin Books Ltd, 80 Strand, London WC2R ORL, England
Penguin Group (USA) Inc., 375 Hudson Street, New York, New York 10014, USA
Penguin Group (Canada), 90 Eglinton Avenue East, Suite 700, Toronto, Ontario, Canada M4P 2Y3
(a division of Pearson Penguin Canada Inc.)
Penguin Ireland, 25 St Stephen's Green, Dublin 2, Ireland (a division of Penguin Books Ltd)
Penguin Group (Australia), 707 Collins Street, Melbourne, Victoria 3008, Australia
(a division of Pearson Australia Group Pty Ltd)
Penguin Books India Pvt Ltd, 11 Community Centre, Panchsheel Park, New Delhi – 110 017, India
Penguin Group (NZ), 67 Apollo Drive, Rosedale, Auckland 0632, New Zealand
(a division of Pearson New Zealand Ltd)
Penguin Books (South Africa) (Pty) Ltd, Block D, Rosebank Office Park,
181 Jan Smuts Avenue, Parktown North, Gauteng 2193, South Africa

Penguin Books Ltd, Registered Offices: 80 Strand, London WC2R ORL, England

www.penguin.com

First published 2013
001

Copyright © Jacky Newcomb, 2013
All rights reserved

The moral right of the author has been asserted

Set in 12.5/14.75pt Garamond MT Std
Typeset by Jouve (UK), Milton Keynes
Printed in England by Clays Ltd, St Ives plc

Except in the United States of America, this book is sold subject
to the condition that it shall not, by way of trade or otherwise, be lent,
re-sold, hired out, or otherwise circulated without the publisher's
prior consent in any form of binding or cover other than that in
which it is published and without a similar condition including this
condition being imposed on the subsequent purchaser

PAPERBACK ISBN: 978–0–718–17683–9
TRADE PAPERBACK ISBN: 978–0–718–17684–6

www.greenpenguin.co.uk

ALWAYS LEARNING   PEARSON

The English word *heaven* is derived from the spelling *heven* . . . and before that *heofon*. The dictionary describes heaven as the home of God, angels and the spirits of the good or righteous, after death.

This book explores heaven as the realms of the souls of the deceased.

With Special Thanks . . .

To Charlotte Robertson, Leah and everyone at Penguin. As always, I also want to say a big thank you to my wonderful readers for sharing their personal and private experiences and for trusting me to deliver them safely and respectfully on to the pages of my books. Without you, there would be no books at all.

To John . . . my husband with eternal patience. I love you very much.

And last but not least, to all my helpers on heaven-side of life for supporting me and guiding me in my work. Even I know I never produce this work all on my own!

I toast you all with a large glass of champagne . . . and, for now, let's just enjoy 'this' side of life!

Contents

Prologue

When I was a little girl, my father was involved in a horrific car accident. Mum was a non-driver and it was difficult for her to get to the hospital with her three young daughters. Occasionally friends would drive her to the hospital and we'd have a babysitter for the few hours she was away. I recall the fear she used to carry on her face, and I was old enough that I understood her difficulties, even though I was just a young girl.

After a few weeks Mum asked if she could bring her little daughters in to visit Dad. 'Yes, of course, young children don't really notice the machines and wires,' she was told by the nursing staff. As we walked into the hospital the full horror hit me. Dad had lost his kneecap; his leg was plastered and hung up in the air from a pulley system attached to the ceiling. He had tubes up his nose, tubes in his arms, wires attached to his chest and sixty stitches in his face. He looked less like my lovely dad and more like a monster from a horror film.

From that night onwards the nightmares began. I regularly woke up in the night, screaming in terror. I was terrified of what had happened and what was to come. My biggest fear was that Dad would die. How would Mum, a non-driver, cope? How would we buy shopping?

How would she be able to work? What if we were ill and she had to take us to the hospital?

I was scared and vulnerable. Our relatives lived a long way away – there was no one to help. In the hospital I sat at the end of the bed, facing away from Dad, too shocked to do anything else, too dismayed to stare into his bloodied face. I daren't kiss him, daren't tell him I loved him; I was too scared to hug him; it took all of my strength not to cry. Dad didn't need me to cry. I wondered, did he himself know he might die? Did he realize how ill he was and how bad he looked? Had they shown him a mirror? Apparently they hadn't . . .

This single experience left me traumatized for all of my childhood and right through my early and middle adulthood. It wasn't until I'd married, had my own children and they were grown enough to live in their own homes that the nightmares that had plagued me for most of my life began to subside. My own children had passed that vulnerable age where, had the same happened to me, they were not old enough to manage. We spent every spare penny on driving lessons and helping them to buy cars. I wanted my own daughters to be able to cope should something similar happen to them . . . it's funny how we are so influenced by our own experiences! Luckily, I don't have the same fears for my young granddaughter; the memories are now far enough away in the past that I can enjoy my life without worrying about what might happen next.

*

Bizarrely, the hospital visit was not the end of the trauma in my life. Years later, Dad had another car accident. This was followed by a perforated ulcer, gallstones, a brain tumour, a stroke and cancer . . . amongst other things. It seemed like my sisters, mother and I spent our whole lives sitting by Dad's hospital bedside, waiting for him to die. At one point or another he was knocking at death's door and then he'd make a dramatic recovery and go and do something life-changing like fly an aeroplane or drive from our Midlands home right down to the south coast! He never stopped amazing us. I remember one occasion in particular when Dad was in a long coma following a series of brain operations. Several family friends and even doctors had given up on Dad. I recall one person saying, 'I'd rather remember Ron the way he was . . .' as if he was on his way out. Yet Dad always seemed to fight back.

My life, and the lives of my mother and sisters, was like a fairground ride: one minute we were up in the air and then we were pelting down a sharp curve and round a steep corner upside down. I felt as if I were always holding my breath, never knowing what was going to happen next. I thought everyone lived their life sitting by the bedside of a loved one for months at a time . . . but, of course, not everyone does. For those of you that have, I sympathize. I can think of no worse way to live your life.

Dad's life of illnesses and accidents set the course for my future career. Worrying for so many years that Dad might die meant I was left with a deep fascination about death and – more importantly – a fascination with the

3

possibility of an afterlife. Was there such a thing as life after death? Could heaven be real? I spent thirty years investigating the subject and later started writing about real-life experiences of the other side, including people's real-life encounters with the spirits of their dead relatives and life-saving experiences with angels. It helped me, and stories of the afterlife comforted me. It gave me hope, and if it did this for me I knew it would help others too.

Strangely, my sisters and I all began having experiences of our own after Dad's brother passed away in his early sixties. Eric was an amazing character: funny, cheeky and much loved. He died way too soon but, strangely, almost right away he started coming back to visit . . . from the other side. Eric, or at least his spirit, was often invited to 'Sunday tea', a family ritual and an occasion when all the family got together at Mum and Dad's bungalow in a pretty English village. After Dad had been so ill, all he wanted was his family gathered around him. Nothing made that man happier than when his girls, and later his grandchildren, came to visit.

'Did someone invite Eric?' was a regular question. We always knew he was there as the lights flickered in response, right on cue!

Several months after the light-flickering began, the doorbell used to ring; it always happened on a Sunday teatime and no matter how many times we'd rush to the door, there was never anyone there. Eventually we resorted to all sorts of tricks: one person would rush to the door whilst another would run to the large window, watching in case any of the local children were playing a trick, messing with the doorbell in some way. There was never anyone there. Eric's ring was always a single *dingdong*, the usual doorbell tone . . . when a living person was at the door, there was a double *dingdong*. He even had his own chime! We never doubted this bizarre ringing was a message from the afterlife.

Eric made great material for my books and when I started writing about our family afterlife experiences and miracle-type afterlife contact stories sent to me from the readers of my magazine column, Eric was often the star. I recall one day chatting to Dad about the subject of my books and explaining that afterlife communication was real. 'In fact,' I suggested brazenly, 'I bet Eric is here right now, listening in on our conversation . . . and probably when I leave he'll make a sign to let us know he is listening.' We both laughed as I leant down to pick up my bag and we stood up as I went to leave. Exactly at that moment, the smoke alarm gave a single bleep and we both burst out laughing once more. In our family, there was no doubt that the afterlife was real, and our relatives who had passed over couldn't wait to rush back and tell us all about it!

So the scene had been set. I wrote book after book that contained real-life angel and afterlife experiences from normal folk living all around the world. After reading thousands of accounts of their experiences I began to notice patterns in their communications and started to learn a little bit about how the whole thing worked. Heaven was real and I felt I was now beginning to prove it!

Ironically, after years of worrying about Dad passing

away, he managed to make it to the age of seventy-seven. I know that if I'd had any idea that his well-worn body would have survived that long I could have lived a life without worry ... but then, would I have written the books I have? Would my interest in the afterlife phenomenon have been there at all? Probably not!

Some part of me knows that my life was pre-planned to a certain extent; all of our lives are. Dad agreed to play his part and I had agreed mine. I felt sure that writing about afterlife communication was my life mission. I had gained such comfort from the amazing afterlife experiences our family had lived through and almost as much again by reading about others' stories of deceased loved ones reaching out from heaven-side. You can read about my personal story, shared bit by bit, in my many books (turn to the back for a full list), if you want to know more.

After Dad eventually passed away he took over from Eric. Dad appeared in dream visitations to each of his four daughters the night he passed away. It was the start of a catalogue of experiences ... enough to fill a book, in fact. Many years later he still visits, and one of my sisters, Madeline Richardson, and I finally wrote a book about what happened to our family, friends and extended contacts after Dad passed on. At the point of writing this book he has now been gone for four whole years ... yet his most recent 'visit' was just this week!

Dad too flickered lights and set the doorbell ringing, but his repertoire was more sophisticated than his brother Eric before him. Dad set off alarms, yes, but he also turned over the television channel and even messed around with the computers and telephones. Maybe the afterlife tricks were performed by both brothers together – I can imagine Eric acting as Dad's 'wingman', pumping up the energy so they could create types of miracle encounters, experiences and visitations for the family to enjoy and share.

Dad worked hard, and still works hard, to show us that life doesn't end at physical death. Dad had died . . . but he wasn't 'dead'! (You can read about his story in our book *Call Me When You Get to Heaven*.)

And so we come full circle. I wanted to write a book where I gave the answers to the questions that I'd wanted to know myself when I first started out. What happens when we die? What is heaven? Is it a real place? Does it exist? I know you'll be blown away by the many real-life stories I have collected for this book. Do you want to know what happens when you pass on? And more to the point, you say, Jacky, how do you know? Let's find out!

To Heaven and Back . . .

'Heaven, the treasury of everlasting life.'
William Shakespeare

Imagine if we knew for sure that death of the physical body was just the beginning of a different life. After all, the newborn baby goes through a sort of 'death' from the womb before being born into our earthly world. The experience is very different to everything it's known up to that point but the new life as a self-supporting human is no less valid than the life it lived inside its mother. It's just a different type of life.

Grief following the loss of a loved one is something we all have to deal with at one point or another. But knowing for sure that life continues on 'the other side' would help more than a little bit . . . wouldn't it?

The fear of death can be very real. Most of us feel comfortable with the thought that we might one day end up in heaven – we just don't want to have to die to get there, right? Yet many have been on the brink of death and come back with reassuring stories of another world . . . a heavenly space. Let's have a look at this in more detail.

The Near-Death Experience

For many centuries there have been fascinating tales from those brought back from death's door. The near-death experience (or NDE) has been experienced by millions, and many of these people have claimed to have seen a glimpse of heaven whilst their physical body was clinically dead. Amongst their stories are declarations of seeing long-deceased relatives and friends standing in front of them; of seeing a tunnel with an extraordinarily bright 'God' light at the end and experiencing the phenomenon of their whole life flashing before their eyes. Many remember lifting out of their physical body, hearing doctors or nurses exclaiming 'We're losing him . . .' and watching as medical staff worked hard on their body below, trying to restart their heart.

Even though there have been many first-person experiences put on record, there are still those in the scientific and medical fields who maintain that near-death experiences do not exist. Thankfully, more recently, researchers claim that there is now compelling evidence – scientific evidence – that proves the near-death experience is a real phenomenon. Many celebrities have talked openly of their close encounters with the other side. Let's have a look at some of these.

Celebrity Near-Death Experience
PETER SELLERS

The late Peter Sellers's near-death encounters are well-documented. Peter had a series of eight heart

9

attacks before he actually died. After one of his heart attacks he talked about the near-death experience he'd had at the time his heart stopped. Sellers explained how he floated out of his body and watched doctors working on his physical body below him. Then he noticed a bright light and said that he felt that the light was God and that real love awaited him on the other side of the light if he were to follow. He recalls seeing a hand reach out to him through the light and he tried to stretch out and grab it; just at that moment the doctors started his heart again and he found himself back in his body with a voice saying, 'It's not time!'

He admitted that when he finally 'came to' he was disappointed not to have been able to pass through the light at that time. It changed him, and as a result of his experiences he was said to have lost the fear of death. Sellers seems to have been through several of the classic signs relating to near death.

The Science Bit . . .

University researchers at the Rijnstate Hospital in Arnhem, Holland, investigated 344 heart patients who'd been resuscitated after experiencing cardiac arrest. The study was headed up by Dr Pim van Lommel. The findings indicated that 62 patients recalled an NDE, which included various phenomena (out-of-body experiences, seeing a tunnel of light and visits from deceased relatives amongst others). Similar findings were made by Dr Sam Parnia at Southampton University. I actually interviewed Dr Parnia for an article many years ago. The studies showed that people who've experienced an NDE have much less fear of death and dying. The fear is of the unknown: if you know what's coming next, you have nothing to worry about!

My own research (although far from 'scientific', I'll admit) indicates the same findings. Although it's common to find the heavenly place a space of deep, profound, unconditional love and, as many say, 'our true home', resuscitation makes the survivor want to live a more meaningful and purposeful existence . . . eventually. Immediately after resuscitation, many feel a deep sadness that they had to come back into their bodies, feeling that they were cheated out of the opportunity of 'going home' . . . but more of that later.

My own interest is purely in the real-life experiences of thousands of people and what we (and I) have learnt from comparing them side-by-side. My studies have covered paranormal experience in many forms (angel encounters, miraculous recovery, out-of-body experiences, afterlife communication, near death, past-life recall, life between lives, etc.). By reading 'around' the subject and covering such diverse topics, I've discovered that the subject is like a giant jigsaw . . . my role has been very much in piecing it all together.

Celebrity Near-Death Experience
KATE SILVERTON

The TV presenter had a strange experience at Royal Ascot, which she believes was as a result of an allergy brought on after eating a prawn sandwich. The presenter shared her story with readers of the *Daily Mail*, and recalls stumbling about as her mouth and tongue began to swell up and she was gasping for air, really struggling to breathe. The presenter said she closed her eyes and found herself sinking into a long dark tunnel. Luckily she was revived by a stranger who was passing by, a lady who'd experienced the same symptoms years earlier. The woman was carrying an EpiPen in her handbag, a syringe containing a single shot of adrenalin, prescribed for patients with potentially fatal allergies. A useful encounter as it was clearly not Kate's 'time'.

I couldn't end this section without including a famous debunker of the existence of life after death. In 2011, physicist Professor Stephen Hawking, who has the debilitating condition motor neurone disease, risked the wrath of religious groups and those with spiritual beliefs all over the world by suggesting that heaven and the afterlife were merely 'a fairy story for people afraid of the dark'. The sixty-nine-year-old caused much debate with his book, claiming that the universe had not been created by God. In an interview he said there was no heaven and our brains switch off like 'broken-down computers' at death!

Lawyer and afterlife expert Victor Zammit says on his website that other 'genius' scientists – physicists, chemists and biologists such as Sir Oliver Lodge, Sir William Crookes, Sir William Barrett and many others – scientifically examined the afterlife. They were men and women of enormous intellectual courage who certainly did not believe in 'fairy stories'. And they ALL decided that the afterlife does exist.*

Celebrity Near-Death Experience
SHARON STONE

The actress had a near-death experience following a brain haemorrhage. Later she talked about what happened to her and said that a giant vortex of white light came upon her before she found herself taking off into a glorious bright white light. She was met by some of her 'friends', she explained, but all of a sudden she found herself right back in her body again.

Facts and Figures

Over half of all Britons believe in the existence of some sort of life after death. Two-fifths of us believe in guardian angels. Some of this group have experienced personal

* Taken from Mr Zammit's website www.victorzammit.com, used with permission.

encounters with one or both types of phenomenon. Around 53 per cent of people believe in 'psychic powers' and as many as one in five of us have actually seen or felt a ghost. One-third believes in heaven and a fifth of us feel we will reincarnate into a new body after our existing physical body passes away.

Many of us believe we've seen, felt, heard or been touched by the spirit of a deceased loved one and are more likely these days to talk about our experience to others. Strangely, after death many of us are looking forward to meeting and communicating with the late Princess of Wales . . . one in five British adults, in fact! Also on this exalted list are Albert Einstein, Marilyn Monroe and Freddie Mercury. Many of us still refrain from sharing our experiences of sensing or seeing ghosts, however, because we fear ridicule.

Celebrity Near-Death Experience
ELIZABETH TAYLOR

The late British actress was once pronounced dead on the operating table following an operation. In an interview on CNN with Larry King, the star described how she met up with the spirit of her late husband, Michael Todd, who'd died in a plane crash. Todd explained that she had more work to do in her earthly life and that she had to go back into her body. Ms Taylor said that he 'pushed me back to my life'.

She didn't talk about it for a long time, she explained, because after telling friends she felt it sounded 'screwy', although later, when the actress worked with people with AIDS, she readily spoke of her experience, telling them that she was not afraid of death because she'd already been there.

Talking to a magazine, the actress shared more of her experience. Mike had told her, 'No, baby. You have to turn around and go back because there is something very important for you to do. You cannot give up now.' She felt that it was literally her late husband's love that brought her back to life.

Ghost, Spirit or Angel?

During these near-death experiences, people often encounter others. Do we understand the difference between a ghost, a spirit or an angel? Here are the classic, most accepted explanations for each of these:

Ghost – a recording (in the same way that voice records on tape) on the atmosphere of an energy (animal or human usually). A ghost has no consciousness and doesn't interact with perceivers. The apparition appears when atmospheric conditions are right and replays. It's common for the replay to be of an occasion of high energy (positive or negative) and 'ghosts' are often seen as wailing and in distress, dead or dying or, occasionally, very happy. It certainly seems likely that these states of high energy were necessary to create the recording phenomenon in the first place.

15

Spirit – a conscious living entity that interacts with the perceiver; recognized as the continuing life force/spirit of a deceased person. The spirit is usually (although not always) connected to the person or place at which it appears. Spirits usually appear with a message, a sign of reassurance or love, or to bring a warning of some kind.

Angel – a being of light, who often appears surrounded by a bright glow or halo; a distinct and separate 'race' or type of being to human souls. Angels were created by God without the free will associated with humankind. They were created with many roles in mind, serving at the will of God. One of these roles is the care of and protection of human beings, and to act as Guardian Angels, regularly being seen during near-death phenomena. Usually appearing as tall, human-looking figures of no gender (neither male nor female), and sometimes with wings and sometimes without. They often appear when we are sick, during grief or distress and during illnesses and accidents, not just 'near death'.

Celebrity Near-Death Experience
DONALD SUTHERLAND

Donald Sutherland, movie actor and father of *24* actor Keifer, almost died with meningitis in 1979.

The actor recalls how his pain and fever seemed to disappear as he found himself floating outside of his body and surrounded by a soft blue light. He then found himself gliding down a long tunnel, away from the bed, before being drawn back to his body again. The actor was later told by doctors that he had died for quite some time.

What is the Soul?

When Dutch scientists weighed the physical body before, during and after death, they noticed a weight loss of $2\frac{1}{4}$ ounces after the physical body died. Is this weight loss the weight of the human soul? Many think it is.

The soul seems to exist as a separate unit from the human body. Anyone that has ever had a near-death or out-of-body experience will tell you that the part they thought of as being 'them' was the part that left the physical body . . . the spirit, or soul. When leaving the body we immediately know that 'we' are the soul, NOT the body!

Our scholarly teachings suggest that 'we' are our brains. Yet this reticular system is just a fancy name for a group of cells in your brain that collect and send out the sensory input from the world around you; everything you feel, see, hear, touch and sense. It's a filter and computer. The brain helps regulate the human body but it's not *you*, it's not who you are – the body is just the home that you live in.

Celebrity Near-Death Experience
BELINDA CARLISLE

Following a three-day 'cocaine binge', the pop star confessed that she saw her own death in a terrifying vision. She found herself out of her body and witnessing herself having an overdose and being found dead in her hotel room. She knew the vision was a type of warning and that if she continued her drug-taking habits she would die. The singer shared her extraordinary warning vision in her autobiography, *Lips Unsealed.*

Why Are We Here? Life Between Life

I'm not suggesting I can offer you the meaning of life in two paragraphs, but I think I now have the answer to the question 'Why am I here?' or 'What is the purpose of my life?' After all my years of research, the simple answer seems to be: we are here to learn and grow (whilst helping others along the way). Our souls come to earth in a human body so that we can experience many different things.

Dr Helen Wambach wrote a book called *Life Before Life*. Over many years she hypnotized people (over a thousand) and took them back to a time when they existed before they were born (before their spirit entered the human body). In nearly every case, people remembered that their soul chose the life they currently lived, including whether they were to be born either male or female (gay, straight or another variation), which parents they were going to be born to and what lessons and problems they were going to live through. Her research suggested that we choose our lives. We pick the hardships and challenges that we are to endure in life!

What's almost more interesting is that people are able to recall existing before physical life. Where were these people during this choosing period? Were they in heaven? It certainly seems like it!

Dr Wambach is not alone in this research; there are many other hypnotherapists who are currently studying 'interlife' experiences (life between lives) by using hypnotherapy. Working independently, results of studies are extremely similar. Yes, sadly, we only have ourselves to blame for the life we have chosen! ☺ It seems that many of us may be over-ambitious in what we feel we'll be able to handle once in a body.

If you want to do more research, other key names in this area include Dolores Cannon and Michael Newton. Or search 'interlife' or 'life between lives' on the Internet. Your local bookshop or library may offer further suggestions for reading up on this subject.

Celebrity Near-Death Experience
GARY BUSEY

The movie star, best known for his role as Buddy Holly in *The Buddy Holly Story*, was involved in a horrific motorcycle accident back in 1988. The actor was not wearing a helmet when he crashed and was flung over the top of his motorbike before landing headfirst on the kerb. As a result of his accident he had a near-death experience, which he later described.

Gary recalls being surrounded by angels looking like big balls of light that floated around him. Best of all, he remembers the lights being filled with nothing but unconditional love and warmth.

So have other people visited the afterlife? You bet they have! Let's have a look at their real-life experiences and examine what this phenomenon might tell us.

Visiting Heaven

'For we know that if our earthly house of this
tabernacle were dissolved, we have a building of
God, an house not made with hands,
eternal in the heavens.'

2 Corinthians 5:1

Heaven is real . . . We know people – many people – have
been there!

What Can We Expect When We Die?

In August 1932, university graduate Arthur Yensen
had an extraordinary near-death experience. During an
afterlife visit he was given spiritual knowledge. Yensen
briefly died during a car crash and his afterlife experience
followed.

Yensen started to pull away from his physical body,
knowing instinctively that he'd 'die' if he did so. All at
once he felt a pain in his heart and he felt his spirit lift out
through the top of his head, with the earthly scene fading
away below him. He found himself in a bright new world;

he called it 'beautiful beyond imagination'. In the distance he could see people dancing with joy and, as they spotted Yensen, they moved towards him. They explained that he was now in the land of the dead, and he felt delighted at his predicament.

One of the group stepped forward and explained that the heavenly realms were a pure place held together by a Master-Vibration which kept the afterlife 'eternal', with nothing getting old or wearing out. After death, he explained, people are drawn together with people of a similar vibration, the highest vibration being the place of love and advanced spiritual development.

Yensen himself became aware that everything in life had a purpose that worked out eventually for the good. He was enjoying the ecstasy of being in the heavenly realms when he was given the news that he had important work to do on earth and he must return to his body. Afterwards, Yensen described his recollection of heaven as: '. . . vivid greenness, its crystalline cleanliness, its newness, its all-pervading music and its overall beauty.'

He was happy sharing his experience with others but it brought him much criticism, especially from the Church. Lots of people were fascinated by his near-death experience and Yensen went on to publish a booklet about his encounters called, 'I Saw Heaven', before finally passing away in 1992. (See 'Further Reading' at the back for details of more stories like this.)

Here is another heavenly visit.

Meditation Visit

My friend's dad had recently passed to spirit and I was sitting in my spiritual circle doing some meditation. I suddenly found myself transported into a wonderful placc. I went up through the clouds and found myself in a spectacular garden. The flowers were amazing, with colours of all shades that you could only dream about. They were so vivid. The flowers themselves were absolutely huge and I mean they were so massive that they filled the borders to the brim with just the flower heads alone!

Next I noticed the grass and it was also huge; each blade was pronounced and the shade of green was intense. While I was looking around in total bewilderment I suddenly saw my friend's dad just lying on the grass. He was lying on his side, propping his head up with his hand; he had his elbow resting on the ground. I went across and sat beside him and we exchanged words, but not through our mouths, through our minds [*telepathy*]. I can't remember the conversation we had but I will never forget the beautiful gift he gave me of seeing heaven. When I feel sad or down I think of that place and it makes me smile inside and out.

Julie, England

The Space Between

So many people these days get the opportunity of peeking through the gates of heaven; imagine if you too could just get a little glimpse of what was on the other side. The space between our world and the next is often shown using some type of symbolism. This varies a lot but common signs on the border crossing are:

- A gateway (the archetypal pearly gates), or a door.
- A river or stream which we cannot cross.
- A bridge (sometimes seen as a rainbow bridge).
- A lake which we (or they) have to row across in a boat (my dad liked this symbol as he was a keen fisherman in life).
- Various things with 'levels' like a staircase, escalator, lift or multistorey car park; our level is lower than their level and they are seen to come down to us when visiting from heaven-side.
- Natural barriers like a hedge. I recall one lady seeing her friend on a heavenly beach.
- Mystical barriers like a vortex of energy or tunnel of light (often seen during the near-death experience, these show the speeding up of the vibration between one realm and the next); sometimes this is described as a type of star-gate or even a cloud of light.

These signs don't indicate heaven but show us the route we'd have to take to visit the other side. We literally have to pass through this border crossing to enable us to reach heaven proper. Tracey was lucky enough to see the stairway symbol in her dream visitation:

Visiting Heaven

When I was around the age of eighteen, my grandfather died. My grandmother didn't cope at all well and seemed to have given up on life. It left me with severe panic attacks. I'd lived with them both since I was six months old and it was terrifying. I kept imagining that I was going to die too; I couldn't tell anyone about the fear I'd been experiencing.

Then one night I felt that I had 'died' when I was asleep in bed; I was shown the most wonderful staircase. It was made of marble and was the most beautiful blue colour. I don't remember seeing anyone at first but I could hear music playing as I began to climb up the stairs. I've never felt such peace as I did that night. For some reason I turned around and wrapped in sheets were four people that had passed away. One was my grandad and one was my other nan. I felt that I had been given a choice to make. Even though I wanted to 'go home', I couldn't leave my grandmother behind. She was already suffering enough. When I looked, I realized I had walked up three steps when I saw them ... there were about twenty altogether so I hadn't travelled very far.

Tracey, England

Here is another sign which indicates the doorway to the other side of life. There are quite a lot of afterlife signs in this particular story so I have left them intact for you to enjoy.

Visiting

When my dad died on 19 January 2004, for several weeks afterwards the lights would flicker and the television would turn itself on and off. The day after he died I had to take my mum into Chelmsford to register the death; we passed a lottery stall and I bought a ticket called 'Pennies from Heaven'. I was delighted when I won £1 so I went back inside the shop and bought another ticket with the winnings. This time I won £5. I always said that if I saw a horse called 'Pennies from Heaven' I would back it . . . so this was close enough!

Each Christmas Dad would buy my mum a box of Black Magic chocolates. They were her favourite, and I love the orange ones myself. Before he died he'd bought her some chocolates ready for that Christmas. It hadn't been opened and when Mum did open it, she said, 'That's funny, there aren't any orange ones . . .' I looked under the top layer and discovered that between the two layers were the four missing orange chocolates! Thank you, Dad!

One day I was just dozing off in the bath when I heard my dad call my name very loudly, waking me up. Maybe he was worried I would accidently go under the water!

My friend's stepdad died the week after my dad and her husband texted me a lovely poem: *don't grieve the faded bloom . . . rejoice in its beautiful flower . . .* or words to this effect.* I haven't been able to find the poem again, but it was pages long on my phone. One day I was distraught and my phone bleeped a message from my dear friend Andria; it just had the first line from this poem, 'Don't grieve the faded bloom'. Then I texted her back and said, 'Thank you so much.' Andria was shocked to get my message . . . she said she hadn't sent any message to me, yet my phone indicated that she had! Was it Dad up to his tricks again?

Then another day the lights were flickering and my son's friend, a scout, said that the lights were spelling out ODD in Morse code. My dad's surname was Oddy, something my son's friend didn't know, so we immediately suspected Dad again! When I went in for an operation a while later, the lights flickered above my head all night in the hospital and days later my son had an operation and the lights also flickered constantly above his bed too. We did find it comforting.

---

* I did a search for this poem myself and I think Jane may be talking about a Russian love poem by Alexander Sumarokov. I could not find the name of it.

My mum changed all my dad's premium bonds a year after he died in January 2005. Her birthday is 11 January and on that day a premium bond came for £50 . . . thank you again, Dad! These little experiences just seem to go on and on. I remember another experience that Mum shared with me. The light in the garage of Mum and Dad's bungalow hadn't worked for years before Dad died. One day Mum wasn't feeling well and she got up to go to the bathroom. As she did so the light came on in the garage, lighting her way to the bathroom!

In another experience, I had a dream that my family was in the nightclub at a caravan park we'd holidayed at in Great Yarmouth. I saw my dad sitting on the balcony above us. He was watching us and then he got up to walk along this long corridor. It had a bright light at the end and even though Dad had his limp and walking stick I was still unable to catch up with him!

Jane, England

Several of my own family members have flickered lights for us after they passed away . . . shame no one knew Morse code, right? What fun we could all have had! OK, now in the next chapter we'll take a look at some more stories about what it's like to visit the other realms . . .

Note

After I finished writing this section I closed down my computer. That night I went to bed as normal. I remember immediately falling into a deep and relaxed sleep. Almost right away I had a dream-visitation experience in which my late father came to visit me. It was completely clear, clearer and more vivid than if he had visited me and I had been awake. I immediately realized that he was 'dead' and that he was visiting me as a spirit from heaven. Although my body was fast asleep my mind was completely awake and aware. Once the visit was over I became fully awake and switched the light on to write down my experience; it was 1.10 a.m. I actually tapped it into my mobile phone which was sitting by the bed – it took me ages to type up with two fingers! Then I emailed the experience to my home computer from my phone. This is what I wrote (I've just added a little more detail):

'Co-incidental' Dad Visit

I was having a normal dream in which I found myself lounging on a bed in a type of bedsit with another female family member in the room on the other bed (I have no idea who this was). Suddenly I looked up and Dad was stood in the doorway of this room. He looked about forty, slim, tanned and with loads of thick hair (he was seventy-seven when he died). In reality he was already thin on top at this age when alive but in the visit he had so much hair it almost looked like a wig! He was wearing light-coloured slacks and an open-necked long-sleeved business shirt, very much the sort of thing he would have worn when he was alive. He looked relaxed like when he was on holiday.

He walked into the room saying, 'Look, I'm here . . .' and had his arms open wide. I reached up and took hold of both of his hands, which were large and tanned and were exactly like they had been in life. He then tried to gently pull his hands away but I wouldn't let go. I knew that if I held on to his hands he wouldn't be able to stay as long to chat to me . . . I think it was a shorter visit because I held his hands but I didn't care. To be honest, I missed his physical touch so much it was just wonderful to hold on to him, even if it was a really brief moment. Dad seemed resigned to my choice – he sat next to me on the bed and I still held on tightly to his hands. I leant over and rested my head on his lap as if I was a little girl, and he stroked my hair.

I told him that I loved him very much and that I missed him; I also told him how wonderful it was to be able to hold his hands again. Dad agreed! Then he started to fade away; it was as if my holding his hands contributed to draining the energy from him, but he didn't mind. I held on to his hands until the very last moment, then I woke up immediately. One minute I was fast asleep and the next I was completely wide awake. As I lay there for a moment I could still feel his hands in mine and I found that I held my hand up to my cheek in the way that Dad used to when he was alive.

It was the clearest, most vivid contact I have ever had from him; so real, and so wonderful.

Strangely, as I typed up this section of the book, my computer made a peculiar noise that I had never heard before. It sounded like a cartoon mouse might do if it laughed . . . and then it did it again. To be honest, it made me jump a little, but when I called my husband in to listen to the noise it just stopped. Within a couple of minutes of him leaving the room the noise came back and it squeaked a couple more times. It was another strange 'coincidence', as these contacts often are. I can't even prove to you that it happened . . . but I know it was real!

Day Trip to Heaven

'Death . . . is no more than passing from
one room into another. But there's a
difference for me, you know. Because in that
other room I shall be able to see . . .'

Helen Keller

My cats often sit on my desk when I am working. The small black cat, Magik, likes to sit on my letter tray, and the big ginger tom cat, Tigger, sits wherever he likes . . . often on the keyboard! They just like to hang around my writing room.

One day when I was working on this book Magik jumped up on to a display cabinet I have in my room. This was unusual behaviour because I have lots of objects displayed on the top, so it's not an easy place for her to jump safely. Next to the cabinet is a tall bookshelf and Magik reached up her paw as if she were attempting to remove a book from the shelf. She actually flicked two books from the shelf, *Life After Loss* by Raymond Moody and Dianne Archangel, and *Companion to Grief* by Patricia Kelly.

If ever I wondered if my spiritual guides helped me to

write my books, this was one of those occasions . . . or if this seems as far-fetched to you as it did to me, even though I witnessed it, let's say it was another one of those 'coincidences'. Perhaps, after all, she was just trying to get on to the shelf and her selection was accidental? I decided that the cat was probably right so I have included a little bit about grief in this chapter.

Visiting Heaven With the Help of a Friend or Relative

Although it's rare, there are those that have visited the other side with a little help from a departed friend or relative. Kathie Jordan, author of *The Birth Called Death*, was a regular visitor to the heavenly realms. Right from the age of seven and up until she was around twenty-two, Kathie's deceased brother Troy would visit her and take her on afterlife 'road trips'. He pulled her soul from her physical body and together the pair would attend lessons in the other realms. Kathie met and worked with various teachers on the other side, including angels and Jesus himself.

Kathie talks about the wonderful love she experienced during these encounters and at one point explains how her deceased brother lifted her in his arms and took her through the tunnel of light. Jesus' lessons were much like those of the lessons he shared on earth, she says.

Here is another story.

Sorry From Heaven

I have lost a lot of people in my life but my experiences have really helped me with my grieving. My partner's grandad died through cancer. Sadly, his mind was affected in his final weeks; he accused me of not liking him, which was not true, and even though I knew this was because of his illness it still hurt me a lot.

After he died I really beat myself up about not forcing myself to make amends. I felt guilty that I hadn't done more to convince him that I did like him. It really bothered me and felt like unfinished business. Then, around six months after his death, I had a dream about him. We were in his kitchen and he held my hand and said, 'Why don't we let bygones be bygones?' He was simply suggesting we let what happened in the past stay there. Then he kissed me on the cheek.

When I woke up I was so relieved and took great comfort in the visit. It really helped me grieve for him in a normal way.

Carla, England

This next experience is relating to a death by suicide (there are other stories on this subject later on in the book).

Chats and Hugs Like the Old Days

Just over twelve months ago my brother committed suicide. It's been a very hard time for me; I was pregnant at the time he passed. Surprisingly, I've been a lot stronger than I thought I would be. My brother Nathan and I were very close and there was only eleven months between our ages.

Two nights after he died, my partner and daughter and I slept in his room. I had lots of thoughts rushing through my head and I kept asking him questions. I was desperate for him to give me a sign that he was OK. At one point I felt my heart was racing like someone was there in the room, and the blind tapped three times. Me being the jumpy person that I am, I woke my partner up and asked him if he'd heard it. He said simply, 'It's a moth.' I checked the window and it was shut. The bedroom door was shut too so I wasn't sure what to make of it. I did wonder, was it Nathan?

I've also had three 'dreams' of Nathan. One happened not long after he died. I dreamt Nathan and I were in a coffee shop but everything was white. He was in his trendy clothes and also wearing his favourite wristband and hat. Before I'd gone to sleep that night I was asking him questions, like *Why?* I wanted to know if he was OK and also felt that I needed to know if he was happy now. In the dream he said, 'I'm OK, and yes, I'm happy.' It seemed hard to believe so I asked again, 'Are you sure?' He did this little laugh like he always did and said again, 'Yes.' I woke up feeling at ease with the whole thing; I felt fresh like a weight had been lifted from my shoulders.

At the time of my second dream I was going through a period where I couldn't make decisions. Again I was having a hard time. This time we were at our old primary school and I was in the school yard sitting down, and Nathan was sunbathing out at the front of the school. He was on top of a truck and he looked at me with his cheeky grin and smiled. Then I woke up, and wondered what on earth the dream was about. [*JACKY: notice how Nathan was 'in the light' and in a different place to his sister, also higher up on another 'level'.*]

In my third dream the family was all together and going for a walk in a beautiful place, I have no idea where it was. Nathan and I were walking behind the rest of the group and together we were chatting about old times. When Nathan got excited he used to talk really fast and he always used to make us laugh when he did this. In the dream I was talking to Nathan in the excited way he used to talk to me and saying, '. . . remember when we did this . . . remember when we did that?' Nathan started crying and gave me a cuddle but then I started crying too and we held each other tightly before I woke up. [*JACKY: Notice the sadness in this dream visit, which sometimes happens in visits from the spirits of people who have taken their own lives; more on this later.*]

I miss Nathan's cuddles very much and I miss him every day. I have to pinch myself to realize he's really gone. Sometimes I still feel him in my room; it's during those times that my heart races and I feel a little scared. I usually ask him to come again another time because I don't always feel ready for these types of visits!

Mel, Australia

Visits to the Afterlife

One of the more fascinating ways that people discover the secrets of the afterlife is when the deceased takes them on an out-of-body 'visit' to the other side. Usually this happens whilst the person is asleep; one minute you're having an ordinary dream and the next a deceased loved one has appeared and seems to lift you up out of your body (like Kathie Jordan experienced with her brother's visits). Often they will hold out their hand to you and you find yourself going on a little unexpected journey!

Our loved ones are interested in showing us where they have gone to and what it's like in their new home. The afterlife is a wonderful place full of beautiful light and vivid colours. Sometimes the 'visit' is brief and at other times lengthy; heaven is always peaceful and beautiful. You'll find these same descriptions appear over and over again throughout the book.

To Heaven on a Motorbike

My grandad passed away some years ago now, twenty-six years ago to be exact. I was ten when he died and I knew he had gone even though I hadn't realized he'd been ill. He had cancer but at the time no one had told me. With no warning, to me he seemed to pass so suddenly. I cannot recall how I knew but the following morning my dad came to collect me from my friend's house and he said, 'We have something to tell you when we are at home.' For some strange reason I said to my dad that it was OK, I knew Grandad had died. It was as if I had connected on some level.

I never got over the grief of losing my grandad; he was more of a father to me than my actual father was, and even eleven years later I was still asking why he was taken from me. Most of my friends' grandads were still alive and it seemed so unfair.

This one particular night, I went to bed as normal. I was now twenty-one years old and had moved out and was living with my fiancé. Grandad appeared to me in a dream. In this 'dream' Grandad came and collected me on a blue moped and we rode for a while but didn't say a word.

Then I started asking questions but there was never a verbal word said to me. I was getting the impressions of the answers in my mind as a sort of telepathic communication. He rode on and we ended at our destination. He took me to a room that was pure white everywhere. There was nothing in this room other than a white circular table. [*JACKY: Notice again here how lots of things are white, because it's easier for the spirits to manifest a simple backdrop. When lots of colours are shown it's normally an outdoor scene where others are present.*]

Grandad then parked the moped against the table and I noticed a lot of details here, such as the colour of the moped (blue) and that it had a basket on the front. When I asked my grandad what he did whilst up in heaven the answer was that he was happy going around the place doing odd jobs, getting things fixed and sorted. [*JACKY: The deceased often indicate that they have jobs or study whilst in these higher realms.*]

I saw that he had things like a hammer in his pocket and he looked happy and exactly how I had remembered him. When it was time for me to go, all I can remember is feeling as though I was being pulled back into 'real time', as though some kind of magnet was pulling me back and I could hear what sounded like autumn leaves crunching when you walk on them. I awoke and felt at ease and I was calm and happy knowing that Grandad was happy.

It was some time later that I spoke about my visit to my mum and my nan, and they confirmed that he did indeed have a moped some years ago when my mum was sixteen. They said he loved doing odd jobs around the house! I didn't know these things about my grandad so it seemed wonderful confirmation to me that the experience was a real one and not just a dream.

Elaine, England

Here is another experience. Although many people are near death when they have their heavenly visits, it certainly isn't always the case (or even often the case). Sometimes we can be overtired, unwell or just very relaxed when a visit occurs. A migraine caused this encounter.

Falling Up to Heaven

I've always had a connection with my guardian angels and I almost weat to heaven once – I've never forgotten my weird experience. I was having a migraine at the time; it was the worst thing I'd ever experienced in my life. Luckily, I'd never had one before and I've never had one since. I was in so much pain and prayed for it to go away. When I lay down with my head under a pillow it wasn't too bad but I started to feel like I was falling UP.

All of a sudden it was as if I had opened my eyes (even though they were closed) and I saw a bright light. I was amongst the clouds and I began to rise faster and faster until what I can only describe as an angel appeared from one of the clouds. I couldn't see her face but she looked a little like me with long hair and my sort of style clothing. She put her hand out and I thought we were going to crash into each other, but instead she said firmly, 'NO!' in such a strong voice that I immediately felt a jolt and began falling back down again.

Then I woke up and for some moments I felt numb, but I'd stopped crying. I was relieved because at least I wasn't in pain any more. The vision intrigued me and ever since my experience I've found myself wanting to know more about heaven and the afterlife.

Nadia-Salvatore (location withheld)

This next experience also contains some 'common' themes. You'll see that the same things come up over and over again; and it certainly helps to confirm that these encounters are real ones.

Beautiful

I went to a place that appeared to be made all of marble; at first I thought it looked like ice. There were marble benches and as I sat down I looked up and there appeared to be no ceiling. It wasn't cold in this place, although you might expect it to be. It was a nice temperature and as I looked around I could see family members who had passed away. There were family friends too, even people who'd died when I was really young and who I had forgotten all about. They each kissed me and I recall that they all looked so young and well. [*JACKY: It's common for the deceased to appear young and healthy when they appear in a visitation experience such as this one.*]

One took my hand and we went to the most beautiful green meadow. It was a green I have never seen before; it was amazing. [*JACKY: People often describe colours that they have never seen on earth. It's possible that these colours do exist on earth but our human eyes are unable to register them as they are outside the visible light spectrum for a human. We know other creatures can see colours that the human eye is unable to read.*]

Joanne (location withheld)

What is it really like on the other side? What do people see when they visit? Here are a few more comments from people who've visited, either by being taken for a visit by deceased loved ones or because they have briefly died before being sent back to their bodies to share their stories. Some of these descriptions will already be familiar to you from the stories we've heard so far:

I was standing in the most beautiful place. There were marble buildings, streets, trees, flowers . . . and my father was standing beside a huge tree, so green that it hurt my eyes with its beauty . . .

And another:

When you die, you feel as if you have woken up for the very first time; to a more real reality than you ever knew before. As the angels took me forward, I saw trees, shrubs and flowers of every colour imaginable; some colours were new and indescribable . . . a waterfall flowed down through the city . . . its walls were made of glittering gemstones. The massive gate was made of a single pearl. As we got closer to the City, I saw that the streets were made of gold . . .

After Rose's heart stopped she went to heaven too:

> It was full of leaves, flowers and birds. And everything was so colourful. The colours were so bright . . .

This next experience belongs to Diane and happened after she nearly drowned:

> A whole new reality was revealed to me . . . but, in this higher vibration, it was more colourful, more beautiful, more amazing. I saw plants, trees, mountains, lakes, animals and shimmering crystal-like buildings, some very large and ornate . . .

Alan's visit to heaven:

> I found myself in a beautiful translucent marble-like building with many beautiful pillars, something like the Greek Parthenon. Many beings were milling about and I felt like I was in a sort of weigh-station or great library or meeting place or place to congregate for special celebrations or events . . .

Some recall the deep sense of love they felt after they passed on. Dean was officially declared dead for one hour and forty-five minutes before he recovered and came back to report on his experience. He recalls moving as fast as he could to be with Jesus. People were praying for him and he was aware of these prayers passing him by as he was on his journey. He became aware of being at the feet of Jesus . . . his soul, not his body. He felt like he was the only person that Jesus loved, as if he were God's only creation at that time.

Next he became aware of deceased family members; generation after generation of people were waiting, 'the biggest family reunion you could imagine,' he said. He was told that we are 'only passing through' on the earthly planet; earth is not our real home. So many people feel that they don't belong on earth! Here is another similar experience . . .

Don was dead for ninety minutes after his truck was hit by a car. He found himself passing through a dark tunnel into the light. He was also met by many deceased loved ones who had passed before him.

I felt loved, more loved than ever before in my life . . . I don't remember what words they spoke. When they gazed at me, I *knew* what the Bible means by perfect love. It emanated from every person who surrounded me.

Taken from the book *90 Minutes in Heaven* by Don Piper

He who has my commandments and keeps them, it is he who loves me. And he who loves me will be loved by My Father, and I will love him and manifest myself to him.

John 14:21

Dianne was electrocuted, after which a near-death experience followed:

I was met by a radiant angelic being who stood before me smiling . . . she was everything I'd ever dreamt an angel would be . . . her love surrounded me, and my spirit was filled with an almost unbearable joy . . .

Vicki is blind but it didn't stop her being able to see during a near-death experience. She has never seen anything, not even light or dark, no visual impressions even in her dreams, but following a car accident she had a near-death experience and 'saw' for the first time. Vicky found she had lifted out of her physical body. At first she recognized her wedding ring which she could see on her body from the vantage point of the ceiling above. Although people were working on her body, trying to bring her back to life, she had no attachment to her physical body and was happy to float up through the ceiling.

Next, she says, she heard the sound of beautiful wind chimes. Once she was in heaven she saw trees, birds and grass amongst other things. She recalls that everything seemed to be emitting love. Like other 'experiencers', she also saw deceased loved ones and beings that were made of light, even though she says she couldn't imagine what 'light' could be like!

Although no words were exchanged, the people seemed to be welcoming her. Next she spotted Jesus, but he told Vicki she had to go back into her body. He explained to her that one day she would be able to return but that she had more work to do on earth, teaching people more about love and being forgiving.

Dianne follows my Facebook page and has been to

heaven on more than one occasion. Here she shares her experience in her own words – her deceased grandfather offers some fascinating insights into life in heaven.

You Can't Come Any Further...

The first time I went 'over' was the day I had my wisdom teeth out. I went into hospital and was put under anaesthetic. I remember walking for what seemed like miles and miles and then I saw a light. I walked towards it and my grandfather stopped me at the end. He spoke to me saying, 'You can't come any further, Dianne, it's not your time.' [*JACKY: 'It's not your time' is the most common phrase when a person is sent back into their body from heaven.*]

I looked over his shoulder and saw a beautiful field of green grass and a wall behind him. We talked for a while about what it was like in heaven and if he was OK. He replied very clearly that everyone else who had passed over was OK, but he didn't feel I was ready to see anyone else at that time. My grandad said that heaven was a quiet place. He explained how the deceased had jobs to do, such as getting people ready to be reborn. He told me that sometimes after people die they don't 'wake up' right away on the other side, and that it may take days or even weeks before they gain awareness once more. He said they can do whatever they like on the other side; my grandad played bowls, which was his favourite thing to do when he was alive. He explained that he comes back to visit us when he can see the living are struggling with life. He is able to offer guidance when he is asked too. [*JACKY: Notice how a wall is seen behind her grandad here, one of the barrier symbols we discussed earlier.*]

The second time I went over I was giving birth to my son. It was about five years ago. I was taken into the operating theatre just in case I needed an emergency procedure. During the birth I just left my body and recognized that I was suddenly in the same place that I'd been all those years ago when I was with Grandad. Everything looked as before: all green, lovely trees and great peace and quiet. I noticed a small wall in front of me. There were also two walls on either side of the smaller one, and I could see the grass beyond and kept thinking how nice it looked. As quick as I had arrived I found myself being pulled back into my body. I felt like I had been sucked back into reality! I then gave birth. [*JACKY: Dianne felt she was sucked back to reality; others have mentioned being attracted back to the body as if it were a magnet. Watch out for other descriptions of this phenomenon in stories throughout the book.*]

The nurse in the recovery room said to me, 'Don't you ever do that again . . . we thought we had lost you three times!' I just smiled and told them that I'd been to see my grandad. Then I burst into tears as I remembered when I'd seen him in heaven as a young girl and for a moment I felt sad all over again.

The third time was just after my godfather Ronnie had passed over. My godmother Betty had been trying to contact him through spiritualists and psychics but at the time I hadn't realized this. I always felt that it was what had prompted my third experience. I found myself back at the same place I'd visited before and once again I saw all the lovely green fields. Ronnie met me at the wall. He looked really healthy and was wearing shorts. My godfather spoke to me but I didn't see him move his lips. He gave me a message to pass on.

'Tell Betty I am OK; better than ever. Now I am not in any pain. Please tell her I will let her know when I arrive OK.' [*JACKY: Notice how Dianne experienced the telepathy that others have talked about.*]

Ronnie hadn't been able to visit Betty this way but she did say that things had been moved around the house and she suspected her late husband was the cheeky culprit!

The fourth time was just after I had fallen asleep on the settee. I found myself back at the same wonderful place and this time the sun was shining. It looked like a lovely summer's day in the park, but no one was about. I remember it as if it was yesterday because it was so lovely and peaceful. [*JACKY: After visiting several times before it's possible that this time Dianne had her visit because she was simply very relaxed. It's not uncommon to visit the heavenly realms if you are experienced at meditation too.*]

I'm not afraid of passing over myself now and am quite looking forward to it. It's like going to a place you absolutely love to visit in life and look forward to going to again and again.

Dianne had brief visits each time. It's like she just reached the gates of heaven (or in this case the wall) and could really only see what was beyond rather than being able to cross to the other realms properly.

It was lovely that she was also given the opportunity of passing on a message for her godmother. The message from her godfather seems to be that he too was only on his way to heaven rather than having arrived at the higher realms; perhaps he was showing her where he was, in the lovely green area, rather than saying he had actually arrived at his final destination. The wall again shows that classic barrier between our realm and theirs . . . a barrier that we are not permitted to pass until it is 'our time'.

Noreen was a little frightened of her contact experience – as many are when visitations happen for the first time. It's encountering the unknown that is scary, but I promise you it gets easier.

Visiting as Requested . . .

My father died in 1986 when I was thirty. I'd helped my mum nurse him in the last few months of his life and I felt really close to him probably for the first time in my life. It was a very stressful time and I really missed him when he passed.

Not long after he died I had a dream that he came to me. I was still in bed in the dream. [*JACKY: Remember I was in a bed when Dad came to me in my latest dream visit – it was as if he was acknowledging that he was aware my body was asleep. Noreen has other similar experiences to my own visitation too!*]

49

My dad was young-looking . . . very handsome. He was wearing a gorgeous silk shirt with stripes of beautiful jewel colours. It felt like I was 'out of my body', looking down at myself in bed. I could see myself and my husband and the colours of the bedding. My father spoke to me, but not with his mouth, with his thoughts, if you know what I mean? He just said, 'You wanted me to come and now you're scared . . .' It felt so real!

Noreen, England

I am often interviewed on the radio and it usually brings a flood of emails through my website. This one was particularly fascinating. A near-death experience was followed by some interesting phenomena; thank goodness a mysterious 'angel' voice was on hand to save her life!

Electrocuted!

I spoke to you on Radio WM a few Sundays ago. My experiences started when I was young. Things would happen that I couldn't explain, such as predicting my mum was going to win a huge Easter egg. I even knew what time it was going to arrive! I also knew that my aunt was going to die but I was told she was going to be OK once she'd died. I was never sure how I knew these things would happen the way that they did.

My dad constantly told me that I shouldn't say such rubbish. Mum would listen to my rambling but she didn't want to upset Dad. For several years I ignored it but still continued to get messages and warnings all the time. Sometimes I'd heed the warnings and on other occasions I'd just ignore the feelings. Sure enough, when I took no notice it was bound to lead to trouble.

On Valentine's Day in 2004 I had a real sign. I was replacing the handle on my washing machine; I knew what I was doing because I'd done it many times before (you learn how when you're on a really limited budget). At the time I was standing in a huge puddle of water and the next minute I was being electrocuted! A massive surge of electricity went through my body; I could see it and felt I was going to die. It seemed to go on for ages and, all the while, my babies were watching it happen. My life passed in front of my eyes and then I remembered something I'd once heard: 'When you die you go to heaven in what you're wearing!' I felt shocked that at the time I was wearing a small pair of pants and a jumper and I felt concerned about what people would think when they saw me!

Next I heard a voice in my head say to me, 'Just let go . . .' But, I thought, I can't! Then something shouted, 'Let go!' and I managed to move my hand. For hours afterwards I could feel electricity still going around me. The house smelt of death and I personally smelt of really badly singed chicken. My body smelt that way for days but at least I was still alive. My son thought it was funny and told me there was 'lightning' around me. All day long I kept hearing angel songs and then I started seeing angel clouds and tiny crystals everywhere (which I collect). These little signs have not stopped since my experience.

I bought my first angel book a week later; I was just 'told' to pick it up. Then in October 2005 my sister and I were seriously attacked in the street by a stranger. I'm not a fighter – quite the opposite – but I was sort of 'shown' (I can't explain really) seconds before it happened and was told we would be OK. I instinctively knew what was going to happen to both of us and where he was going to hit us. With 'help', I managed to protect my sister and our children. We should have been worse off than we were and afterwards we both felt like we'd been run over by a steamroller, yet the assault left us with no injuries . . . nothing. Luckily, the man was caught and he pleaded guilty to the charge.

Now my house is full of angel cards, angel books and crystals. If I see one I find I have to buy it. I also have an angel room in my home. Some people say I shouldn't keep going on about angels but I just can't help it! I am lucky and blessed to have such beautiful and amazing friends from the other side. They call me the 'Angel Lady' where I work but I tell them no, you're the only Angel Lady, Jacky!

Cherrie, England

Finally, here is a classic visitation-type experience which shows all the signs . . . I'll explain them to you after you've read the story.

Tickling Dream?

Hi Jacky, I felt I had to write to you. I've recently read a couple of your books and found them interesting, I especially liked the book you wrote with your sister about the loss of your dad and the afterlife experiences you'd had.

I lost my own dad in February, about a month ago. After a long illness he died of cancer at the age of ninety-five. Last Friday I had what I could only label a visitation experience. It must have been in the period between shallow sleep and waking up. I was in a white corridor and my dad walked towards me wearing a beige raincoat (I don't remember it in life, perhaps it was one of his favourites and something he'd owned when I was too small to remember!). He took both my hands and put one arm around my waist. I felt an absolutely overwhelming feeling of love and elation. I said to him, 'How are you?' and he replied, 'Fine.'

We walked quite quickly because he seemed in a hurry; he was definitely on his way somewhere and he said something like, 'We must get on.' I am very ticklish around my waist and I could feel his arm tickling me, so I wanted to break away but on the other hand I didn't want to leave his side. The tickling became absolutely unbearable so I did break away and I woke up so fast (it normally takes me ages to even open my eyes). It was almost like someone had plunged me into cold water, I was so awake.

I remember saying out loud, 'My God, that was the most AMAZING experience.' It was definitely not a dream. I dream a lot, and in colour, and they are never anything like that!

The odd thing was that I was suffering a bit and had been missing him earlier that night before I went to sleep. I'd asked for him to come and show me how to move on in my life as you had suggested in one of your books. I had also been offered a job and I didn't know what to do. I was feeling very sad, very confused and quite unsettled and I really wanted advice and guidance. Actually, I still don't know what to do about that job because I never had the chance to ask Dad, but I think Dad saying, 'We must get on,' suggests that he wants me to move ahead and go for it.

I felt like Dad was off somewhere for some fun, but just popped back to reassure me. I have felt fabulous since then, and after seeing him deteriorate in our world and die in a lot of pain it was so fantastic to know he is free of pain and suffering in the place where he is now.

Thank you for your books, Jackie. I don't think I would have had these experiences without reading your work. I don't think I am especially spiritually receptive but you have really helped me to understand that this world isn't the end. I cannot believe for one moment that what happened to me was just a dream.

Simone, England

Deceased spirits can interact with us physically – hold our hand, place a hand upon our shoulder or hug us, for example. When the departed visit us in dream-visitation experiences, though, they usually discourage touching; not because they don't want us to reach out to them but because it takes away the energy they use to hold form (like my own experience where my late father faded away fairly quickly after I insisted on holding his hands). In other words, if they touch us they might fade away, turn 'black and white' or become completely invisible to us.

I have covered the appearance of the deceased in visitations in some of my other books (including *Angels Watching Over Me* and *Dear Angel Lady*) but briefly let me share a few points again here.

- The deceased often look younger when they appear to us in dream visitations (if they died older), or the very young can appear older (up to the age of thirty).
- They can 'grow up' or stay the same age . . . the choice is theirs.
- If they were sick when they died they will likely appear well again (although a series of visitation dreams may show the deceased sick at first and gradually getting better and better).
- They usually appear without their earthly props (no need for false teeth, glasses, walking sticks or wheelchairs as the body is whole as a spirit).
- As before, a first visit may show them *with* their supports . . . but that is for the benefit of us

recognizing them. My dad (who'd used both walking sticks and wheelchairs in the years before he passed on), used to dance, jump and skip in dream visits! But sometimes he appeared with his 'trademark' glasses . . . just for fun!

- If they died with grey hair they'll likely appear with their younger hair colour.
- If they lost their hair it will probably be full and lush in a dream visit.
- The sick will appear glowing with health and vitality (a phrase that people share with me over and over again).
- If the departed had mental or physical illnesses in life, these gradually fade away on heaven-side.
- Sometimes the deceased appear with other deceased relatives (including young child relatives) to show that these other family members are taken care of.
- They might also appear with pets, angels and spiritual guides.
- Sometimes the deceased bring other souls with them as 'gift' visits for us and at other times the visitors are purely with them to help 'hold' the energy long enough for your relative to show their face.

Now let's look a little more at what it's like to take a trip to heaven because of illness or accidents and so on . . . and what it's like to be sent back to earth again!

One Foot in the Door

'To everything there is a season, and a time
to every purpose under the heavens.'

Ecclesiastes 3:1

Being Collected and Escorted 'Home'

On the verge of death it's common to see deceased loved ones, and even to have loved ones come to collect you to take you to the heavenly side of life. I remember my dad telling me, shortly before his own passing, that his grandfather and two aunties had come to collect him one night; he was sleeping soundly in his bed at the time. Dad turned them down – 'No, thank you . . . I'm not ready to die yet!' – even though he was unwell at the time. He lived just a few weeks longer, having one last family Christmas, and finally passing on the following February.

I always wondered who had come to collect him the second time. One night after he died, Dad appeared to me in a dream visitation. I asked him, 'Who came to collect you when you passed over for real, Dad?' This time, he told me, he was met by his late father, whom he hadn't

57

seen for seventy-five years. My grandfather had passed on when Dad was just a two-year-old boy, yet in the dream Dad told me that he recognized his late father immediately! What a comfort it is for us and the deceased to know they are being taken care of, collected and shown the 'way home'.

Nurses, doctors and care workers who are close to the dying often share their stories with me. I've heard amazing tales of the dying who, having been unable to move for many weeks due to their illness, suddenly sit up and smile or wave at some unseen visitor in their final moments. If you visit a dying person, maybe you'll be privileged to hear some of their stories or communication. 'Grandad's been here today . . .' they'll say, or list other deceased family members or friends. Sitting with one foot in heaven and one foot on earth, the other realms seem very real . . . because they are. These stories can be of great support to those watching their loved ones slip away from them. To know for sure that the deceased don't 'disappear' into oblivion – to have a little insight into where they are going next and with whom – well, it's such a relief.

When we lose a loved one to physical death it brings up all sorts of issues: we remember others who have passed before and we worry about what might happen when our own time comes. It can be particularly difficult if your family's belief system doesn't support continuation of the life of the soul . . . yet whether you believe it or not, it doesn't mean you are any less likely to have afterlife contact or experience near-death phenomena!

Do angels come to collect us when we pass over too? Many people see angels during their final days and weeks on earth, as well as their passed-over family members. This family certainly felt their loved one was talking to angels. I'll let them explain their story personally.

Seeing Angels?

Mum and I had been staying with Gran during the month prior to her passing. Gran was very frail and no longer mobile but we found comfort in staying and always had a feeling of a protected presence with us in my gran's bedroom. Gran used to ask us if we saw 'all the people coming out of the walls' and asked, 'Who are all the people walking out of the walls?' Another night she asked, 'Who is that man standing at the bottom of the bed?' and she frequently pointed to the top right-hand corner of the bedroom ceiling, asking, 'Can you see them?' She would lie for hours just staring and smiling at this corner.

Sometimes we'd be walking up or down the stairs and would hear Gran having a conversation with someone, laughing and chatting away, although no one was physically there. Although very frail, my gran was lucid and orientated and not on any medication that would alter her state of mind. After reading your books my mum and I found great comfort in all of this as we felt my gran was being protected and watched over by the angels. Through the help and guidance of your books my mum and

I were not afraid of this, although when my brother heard my gran speaking of these people he felt a little startled; he didn't believe in the phenomenon as we did.

Mum and I stayed with Gran on the Sunday before she passed and Gran was sitting up speaking to us. Before we left she gave us a big kiss and cuddle. At this point I thought to myself that this was the last kiss I would have from my gran – for some reason I just had that feeling. I didn't say anything to Mum at the time, though, because I didn't want to upset her.

We left on the Monday afternoon when my aunts arrived and we returned on Tuesday evening to stay overnight. Gran had deteriorated rapidly and was unable to communicate with us. She did hold on to our hands from the moment we arrived to the moment we left though. Throughout the night both my mum and I were aware that the angels were coming for Gran soon. There were many unusual events that night, and after reading your books we were aware that these might have been signs from the angels.

Gran had now been put on antibiotics by her doctor and her normally high blood pressure had been low. Due to this we'd been checking her temperature and blood pressure frequently. At approximately 5.00 a.m. on Wednesday 31 August my mum and I attempted to check my gran's vitals and the thermometer was reading 'MEM' and the blood-pressure machine stopped working. At this point I thought it was a sign but again I didn't say anything to my mum as I did not want to upset her.

All of a sudden, Mum and I started finding several small dainty feathers all around Gran's bedroom. These feathers were all identical in appearance and there were so many. When Mum or I popped out to the toilet downstairs, there'd be none around yet it was inevitable that when we came back into Gran's bedroom, more of the same type of feathers would have appeared in abundance. Feathers we have found previously have all been different shapes and sizes and we were mesmerized by all these beautiful, small identical feathers, almost as if they had been placed around the room for us to find.

My aunt arrived at 11.00 a.m. and Mum and I left. We both tried to get to sleep when we arrived home, although every time I closed my eyes I could hear Gran's voice in my head. Mum was unable to sleep at all, and then at 1.00 a.m. we received a phone call asking us to go to Gran's house immediately. It was the longest drive of my life, a ten-minute journey that felt like hours. Shockingly, when we arrived we discovered that Gran had already passed over. We never found any of the small feathers at this point, though I turned round after asking the angels to watch over my gran and found a large white feather at the bedroom door. I believe this was a sign she had been collected safely by the angels.

After many tears and despair during the day my mum and I both relayed to one another that we were thinking the same about my gran kissing us on the Sunday; both of us had experienced the same strong feeling that the kiss would be our last one. We had both felt that the thermometer and blood-pressure machines not giving readings had been a sort of sign too. Even now, Mum and I – and even my brother – still find these small dainty feathers; they're all identical in appearance even though we find them in many different places. Mum and I both believe these feathers are gifts from my gran and it's wonderful to think that in some way she might still be around us.

This isn't the end of the story though. My gran lived in her house for fifty-four years and it was sad to let it go. The house had been cleared by other relatives, but the day Mum and I arrived at the empty house we went to her bedroom and discovered it was full of feathers again! I collected all the feathers and when I got home I counted them. There were fifty-four feathers in total, the same amount of years my gran had lived in the house . . . a strange coincidence, I thought. That night I was sitting speaking to my mum in our kitchen and a small card which hangs on the wall fell at our feet. When we lifted it and read it, we noticed the words 'Hang in there'; this gave us great comfort that the angels and my gran were with us, supporting us during this difficult time of mourning.

Gran now regularly appears in my dreams. I am having a lot of trouble with bullying at work (it's being formally investigated). When I was made aware of the investigations I became frightened and uptight, and last night my gran appeared in my dream telling me to ignore them all. She said to me, 'You're better than them, you don't need to fight, darling,' then she gave me a warm cuddle which felt so real. When I woke up I felt as if I had literally just been speaking to my gran and cuddling her. I found great comfort in this.

Mum and I would never have been able to identify any signs from the angels or my gran, and most importantly would not have been able to cope with the loss of my gran, had we not read your wonderful books. My dad and brother, who were both sceptics, are now aware of the signs, and when they find feathers they too believe they are from Gran. We feel this is good for my dad, who's dealing with terminal cancer; it helps him to cope with his own illness and mortality.

(Name and location withheld)

That story was so touching that, like many that are sent to me, it brought tears to my eyes. Feathers are such a common afterlife sign and many people now discover little white feathers in response to their need for comfort and afterlife support during their grief. Have you ever found a white feather? I have a little angel pot at home in which I collect the feathers and once it's full I pass them out to strangers who look a little sad or in need of comfort. I carry them around in my purse and it's surprising how often I have to dip in there for little angel signs. Maybe you feel drawn to doing something similar?

Here is another amazing story about a woman being collected. The experience had by the daughter also acted as a useful warning sign too.

Dad Comes to Collect Mum

You have been a great support to me since I lost my dad in May 2010 and I thank you for your books, which have been really comforting to me.

I would like to tell you about an experience that I had whilst on holiday five weeks ago. My mam had been heartbroken since our dad died because they had been married fifty-six years, and she could not get over losing him. It was not unusual for me to dream about my mam because I was so worried about her. One night I was dreaming about my mam and this time it was a little different. She was in a field playing with children when all of a sudden my dad appeared in the dream. When I asked him why he was there he told me that he was waiting for Mam. However, in the dream, Mam was not aware that Dad or I were watching her.

The following week, I came home to find that my mam was in hospital after a serious fall; it happened because she'd had heart failure, and she was very ill. On Thursday 8 September my mam started talking to my late father and her mother. She told me that they were in the hospital room with us. I felt like I was listening in on one half of a conversation because Mam then told whoever she was talking to that she was coming soon. She explained to me that she could hear children in the room, which was strange because it reminded me so much of my dream.

Mam smiled, then kissed the air before she turned to me and said, 'Now if I die, I die.' It was like she was preparing me. I lay on my mam's bed with her and cuddled her throughout the night and she passed away peacefully the next morning. As a family we are all heartbroken at losing both our parents in less then fifteen months, but we are sure that they are now reunited. I know that Dad came to collect Mam on the Thursday night, because I could feel a pressure when Mam died, as though someone was standing over me; I was unable to lift my head up to look behind me.

Anastasia, Wales

Isn't that an amazing story? It must be wonderful to be able to listen in on this special conversation with heaven! Being close to death, or knowing that you are dying, is a scary thing . . . for everyone. No one actually wants to die, do they? The really weird thing is that we are all dying, from the moment we are born; the difference is that most of us don't know when and where. It's true, of course!

Your beliefs can be of the most enormous comfort . . . unless your belief is that once you die you cease to exist. For many years we have had to rely on faith alone – these days, the truth about what happens next is just there, waiting for us to discover it. Our physical bodies do expire, that's true. The good news is that our personality, our energy – that part of us that makes us 'us' – continues to live and exist in another form. People all over the world who have passed on can't wait to come back and let us know what happens next!

I miss my late father so very much but the thought that he'll be waiting to collect me when my own time comes is fantastic. (Strangely, exactly as I typed that sentence my mobile phone rang as if in agreement. It was a text message from someone I didn't know, sent in error, saying, 'Hope you had a nice Christmas . . .' (it's Boxing Day as I sit here writing). It's probably another one of those 'coincidences', right? Ha ha!

Here is another great story from my letter files; it's about being collected from the other side too, and has a fascinating afterlife contact. These experiences are so reassuring, aren't they?

Collected

I've been reading your books for some while now and I find them fascinating! I had experiences myself but until reading your books I didn't understand them.

In 2001 I was married to my ex-husband and his father died very sadly at a young age. He was just fifty-eight and passed over with cancer. He was such a nice man who loved his family. Before he died he told me he wasn't scared of dying because he'd already seen his late mother waiting for him at the end of his bed. The experience happened before he became really ill and before he was on drugs for the pain.

The day before his funeral his body was brought up to the family home. We were able to visit him and say goodbye. My husband and I went home afterwards and his mother and sister stayed at the family home that night. My sister-in-law woke in the night after hearing a loud banging on the wall. It was coming from the room that the body was in! My mother-in-law had heard the noise too and, when they looked at the clock, they realized it was the time my father-in-law always got up for work on his farm! Luckily they weren't too scared by it all.

Dina, England

It's true that some contact signs are more than a little terrifying!

Not Your Time

You don't have to be near to death to see deceased loved ones; they sometimes appear when we're unwell or unconscious too. Rebekah's deceased family were waiting not just to meet her but to send her right back into her body again.

Seeing Deceased Relatives

I have many stories I could tell you; some are just little memories and others may be moments of coincidence . . . or not! This particular event happened, if I remember rightly, in 2001. I won't bore you with all the silly details but my partner and I lived in our home with our three young boys at the time.

One day my sister was visiting and I had just popped to the loo. I remember feeling unwell and then all I could see was pure white everywhere. [*JACKY: Notice that pure white again!*] I saw my grandfather's face right in front of mine (he passed when I was just three years old, and we were very close). My grandmother was standing just behind my grandfather. He was telling me I would be OK and that I must go back as it was not 'my time'. He kept repeating that my babies needed me and that I had to go back. [*JACKY: the deceased often use this trick to help send us back to our bodies. They tell us that we are needed on earth and show us images of those who would be devastated if we were to leave our bodies for good. Thinking of the living helps to draw us back to the physical body . . . like the magnetic experience people talked about earlier in the book.*]

As I looked over my grandfather's shoulder I could see a very big congregation of people, most of whom I recognized as family. I can still remember wanting so much to go and see them, and then as I heard my grandfather talk for the last time I could hear what sounded like my partner, but his voice was very distant. I opened my eyes and discovered that I was lying on my bathroom floor with my partner's face in front of me, just as my grandfather's had been moments before. He was distressed and asking me not to leave him, and telling me he and the boys loved me. [*JACKY: During times of 'near death' the dying person can often hear the voices of the living, and the requests and prayers of the living can also act like a magnet to draw the soul back to the body . . . worth remembering!*]

I was taken by ambulance and admitted to hospital, where the staff said they didn't know how I was still alive. One nurse even commented that I looked so white she had thought I was dead. They found I only had 5.6 pints of blood in my body and they gave me a blood transfusion. I have always felt that my family in the afterlife saved my life that day. They sent me back to be with my family until it really was 'my time'.

Rebekah, England

I'm sure Rebekah is right!

Go Back to Look After Your Son

In the summer of 1992 I was on holiday in Greece with some friends. One day on the way to the beach I was walking with my friend's mum when a motorbike with two men on it knocked me down on the ground. It was on a wide road but there were no footpaths so we'd had no choice but to walk along the roadside.

I'd been pushing my son who was four years old, almost five, in a buggy. I actually don't recall any of this other than what I was told much later. My friend's mother told me that the bike came up behind us and literally tossed me up and over the top of the buggy. The buggy, with my son in it, was somehow pushed out of the way, although it did turn over. When she went to check on me, she said my body shook and then nothing . . . My son did not have a mark on him!

She tried to feel for a pulse but couldn't find one so she rushed off to get help and stopped the first car she saw. Strangely, the people were English and the man was a doctor! She explained in a panic what had happened and, terrified, she told him that she thought I was dead. The doctor rushed over to where I was lying and he tried to resuscitate me. Again, I have no memory of this part of the experience.

In the meantime I found myself in a completely different world. I was in a wonderful – and what I can only describe as dark – place, which was warm and felt like nothing I have ever experienced before. It was so peaceful and welcoming. I wanted to stay where I was but someone was telling me it was not my time. I couldn't see who it was (maybe my mother, who had died when I was only a child?). They kept telling me I had to go back. I begged to stay as the feeling was just so lovely, I felt so warm and safe, but they insisted and kept reminding me that as a single parent my son needed me.

It was only at this point that I realized where I was – not on earth (though I was not sure exactly where I was). I had no concept of time or place and no memories of any sort until my son's name was mentioned. The feeling was so seductive that I begged for one more minute in this peaceful place but I was told *No, you have to go back now*. I came round with the doctor slapping me and shouting for me to wake up. He took me to the hospital in the car he was driving; I have no idea how long all this took because I kept passing out. I stayed in hospital for four days because I had a head wound that required stitches. When I got home from the holiday and went to my own doctor I remember him saying that with the position of the wound on my head, I was lucky to be alive. To this day I don't really understand what the dark peaceful feeling was, but I have never forgotten that I went there and how amazing it felt.

I've just finished your book about the experiences your family went through when you lost your own father and it got me thinking about this. It was a very comforting read as, although I'm interested in the afterlife, it does scare me. Your book took the fear factor out of it.

Majella, Ireland

The Near-Death Review

Gail's trip took her a little bit further along the heavenly route, as you'll see in this next story!

Having a Near-Death Review

I took some antibiotics but I didn't know that I was allergic to them. Almost right away I started to feel really ill and couldn't breathe. I think it was at that point that I had a type of near-death experience.

I didn't see heaven (I don't think so anyway), but I watched my life happen in front of my eyes. It was like watching everything on a film and it seemed to start from when I was around five years old . . . all the important parts I was able to witness. I somehow 'came to' enough to telephone the doctor. The next thing I recall is that my neighbour called round to the house and was able to help me. Afterwards she said that she didn't know why she'd felt compelled to visit me at that moment but I'm so grateful that she did. She took care of my three-year-old son and my daughter for two days whilst I was in hospital. I guess this time it just wasn't *my* time . . . thank goodness.

Gail, England

Lessons of the Near-Death Review

A 'near-death life review' is one of many things that can be experienced at the point of physical death. When people say 'my whole life passed before my eyes', they literally mean it. The life just lived is often witnessed, as with Gail's experience, as if watching it unfold on a screen. The 'life movie' can speed up and then slow down when important aspects need closer review. The humdrum aspects of life are irrelevant and only those experiences that help with learning are examined closely. If there is an aspect where we were perhaps particularly kind or loving, or extra mean, then these are the areas we have to examine more closely, or zoom in on. Not just to look at but also to sense and feel the experience all over again.

People say that when they witness the life they have been living in such detail it makes them consider how they might do things differently in the future. For example, if there were consequences to our actions (perhaps we helped or hurt someone) then these need to be given extra attention. I always think that the near-death review is such a gift (and people have confirmed this). I haven't had one myself but like to learn from the example of those that have. We have a choice each and every day how we live our lives. When your time comes, do you want to watch a movie in which you were uncaring or cruel, or one in which you were kind and loving? I know which one I'd like to watch!

If you've done unkind acts in the past (and which of us

hasn't?), just know you are only human. Try and work hard every day to live your best life from now on . . . make the 'nice' you be the one that shows its head each day when you get out of bed (or at least for most of the time anyway!).

Quick Trip to Heaven in the Dentist's Chair

Years ago, many dentists used laughing gas (nitrous oxide), an inhalation anaesthetic. My mother was terrified of the dentist, a trait she passed on to us, and we went to our particular dentist because he used this form of anaesthetic rather than a needle in the mouth.

I recall two occasions when I had this treatment and both times I found myself out of my body and travelling down a tunnel with a bright light at the end. After years of investigation I discovered the familiarities with traditional near-death experiences. (Although I don't feel I was in any danger at any time, it did take some time to bring me back to full awareness!)

In the first experience I felt wonderful and at total peace. I was pulled in the direction of the bright light and was aware that others were in the tunnel with me all going in the same direction. One couple were dressed in competitor's-style ballroom dancing clothes and were literally dancing their way along the tunnel. The tunnel was also spinning towards the light and was getting faster and faster the further along I went. I totally enjoyed the experience and when I had to make another trip to the dentist I was really looking forward to going through the experience again.

The second 'trip' was quite different, sadly. I still saw the tunnel but this time a large 'monster blob' type of creature was barring my way and, rather than floating along the tunnel in the peaceful way I had previously, this time I was trying desperately to backtrack and return to the beginning . . . I did not want to go into that light! I felt relief as I heard the dental nurse's voice calling my name and urging me back.

I wonder if my experience the first time had been too exciting. Maybe if I had reached the end of the tunnel I might have found I was dead! I have wondered in the years since if the 'monster' vision occurred to protect me from floating too far towards the light. Of course, I have no way of knowing, but I've been interested to read about other people's dentist experiences ever since. Here is another story:

Dentist Heaven Trip

When I was a young boy of about eleven years old, I had to have some teeth extracted. Dad and I went along to our usual dentist and, surprisingly, I recall my experience very clearly even after many years. I was accompanied by my dad, and I remember sitting in the dentist's chair; the room was stark, decorated in a pale green emulsion. I was given an anaesthetic and I remember the mask went over my face and I breathed in the nitrous oxide.

Right away the room began to spin. I felt that I was travelling through a bright tunnel of light; the journey seemed to take the briefest of time before I found myself in a bright, grassy place with three men. I wasn't afraid, I felt awesome love and peace; I felt safe. I clasped one of the men's hands for reassurance as I felt like I knew who they were. Even though I had never met them before, as far as I know, they seemed totally familiar to me.

During my experience, time seemed irrelevant, and I certainly didn't want to leave and come back into my body. Then, as though from a great distance, I heard my name being called and a voice told me, 'You have to go, it isn't your time.'

Reluctantly, I let go of the man's hand as the voice in the distance became more and more insistent. Next, I found myself being drawn back through the tunnel. I could feel the wind moving past me and I felt myself cough as my lungs began to fill with air once more.

My dad was holding tightly on to my hand and I heard the dentist say that he thought he had lost me . . . although I didn't understand what he meant by that at the time.

I believe the experience gave me a brief glimpse of heaven, and for the shortest time I had the sensation I was with God. Since then, I have had several spiritual experiences which remind me that I have to share my heaven experience with others. I have never been able to replicate the experience, even though I have wanted dearly to return to that place.

Throughout my younger years I was aware that the three men watched over me still. One night I remember waking and seeing them gazing through my bedroom window; they were silhouetted through my curtains.

Michael, Scotland

We've seen some fascinating glimpses of the other realms ... now let's have a more detailed look at some visits from heaven – real-life encounters with those on the other side. They have a lot to teach us ...

Call Me When You Get to Heaven

'Perhaps they are not stars, but rather openings
in heaven where the love of our lost ones pours
through and shines down upon us to
let us know they are happy.'

Eskimo proverb

Visits From the Other Side

There are numerous books written on the subject of contact from the afterlife, including many books I have written personally. My books contain stories of spontaneous visitations, real-life visits from the deceased, where they visit us directly rather than through an intermediary (a psychic medium). These experiences take on many forms, the spirits creating many different types of phenomenon to let us know they are around; some are subtle but many are not. Our deceased loved ones have to ensure they are never frightening (although sometimes they might be, it's never their intent). Visiting us from the afterlife and making our grief worse, or effectively 'haunting us', is not permitted!

Signs include a wide range of encounters, including:

- Animals (both wild and domesticated, e.g. pets), acting in unusual ways. Sometimes a favourite animal of the deceased will keep appearing in some form.
- Birds tapping on the window, sitting on your hand or drawing especially close to you (most regular of which are robins and humming-birds . . . depending on what part of the world you live in!).
- Butterflies and dragonflies (occasionally moths) – appearing in unusual places at a time of year when they really shouldn't be around. Butterflies appear a lot at funerals, flying down into the coffin, travelling along in the funeral cars, etc.
- Rainbows – one story someone shared with me even had the rainbow appearing to 'end' right on top of a coffin. On the day of my dad's funeral a rainbow appeared in the sky, the end of which seemed to go right into the family bungalow.
- Pennies – coins appearing out of thin air.
- Crystals – again, dropping on to the floor and materializing from nowhere. I was with a friend shortly after Dad passed on. We were actually at a crystal warehouse (crystal wholesaler) when a piece of crystal fell on to the shelf in front of us – there were no shelves or crystals above the shelf where this 'chip' appeared so it was a little strange that it just bounced on to the shelf . . . it

79

sounded like it had only dropped about thirty centimetres or so.
- Feathers – mainly white and all different sizes, some tiny fluffy feathers and others large white feathers (from swans?). Feathers always appear in a timely fashion and always in response to a request or need for a sign. You don't need to look out for white feathers . . . they find you!

More recently loved ones seem to manipulate electricity or use our modern devices to indicate their presence. This includes:

- Leaving messages on answerphones or phone-recording devices.
- Hearing voices of the deceased on baby monitors (chatting to their new grandchildren, children or siblings maybe?), or other recording devices.
- Appearing on photographs (sometimes as orbs/balls of light, but at other times appearing as if they had literally stepped into the photograph).
- Manipulating clocks (setting off alarms, changing the time, stopping the clock or watch at the exact time they passed on).
- Messing with computers (photographs appearing spontaneously on-screen, 'email' arriving from their old account – usually with no message attached, or in my case, a file name changed to a

word that had great meaning for my late father and no meaning to me!)

- Music (their favourite song plays on your radio, CD player or other player just as you were thinking of them and often when the player hadn't been set to play – or wasn't even plugged in . . . now that's spooky!).
- Music boxes seemingly winding themselves up so that they play spontaneously at an appropriate moment. Other clockwork and wind-up toys which seem to speak to you or sing to you in response to a request or question.
- Pagers, tape recorders and telephones picking up voices, bleeping when the deceased person's name is discussed, etc.
- Televisions – my late father once turned over the TV channel to indicate his favourite song was playing. I once had a TV switch itself on when it was unplugged at the wall. Other books of mine have stories where a specific television pro- gramme had recorded (one in which maybe the deceased appeared). Feeling sad over Christmas without Dad, I noticed that a series of fishing programmes had been recording spontane- ously . . . no one in our house likes fishing but Dad used to love it!
- Walkie-talkies – again, picking up the voice of the deceased saying single words, usually 'hello', or 'Tell [*fill in the blank*] that I am OK' or just saying your name.

Many have had these encounters with the other side, those 'something strange happened' moments. The experient (the one with an experience) is usually left in no doubt that the afterlife is real, that it exists in some way and that their loved ones survive death, but unfortunately those with no contact are the ones that find it hardest to believe, and that is understandable – we are only human, after all! (Or are we? But that is a whole other book . . .)

These life-changing encounters with the other side often leave the living feeling comforted and healed. Here are some more true life stories.

Heaven Calling

My mother-in-law's partner was in hospital and had been ill for about two weeks. His name was Bob and he reminded me of my grandfather. He had the same white hair and it was cut in much the same way too. He also looked a bit like my grandfather and he was a nice old gentleman whom I cared a great deal for.

Anyway, he'd been taken into Basingstoke hospital and no one knew what was really wrong with him but he went downhill quite quickly. We are quite a large family and had supported him through his troubles and visited him in hospital too. My husband and I had a special bond with him and enjoyed his company, often going out with him and my husband's mother.

One morning when we were fast asleep the telephone rang. It was 6.15 a.m. We hadn't been expecting a call at that time of the morning and my husband answered the phone but no one was there, just an empty sound, and then the phone went 'click' like someone had put it back on the receiver. We returned to our slumber and thought no more of it.

At around 9–9.15 a.m. we had a telephone call from my mother-in-law saying that Bob had died that morning, and when my husband asked what time she said '6.15 a.m.' We were stunned.

My husband, who is a bit of a sceptic about these things, was gobsmacked and his face was a picture as this was the exact time we had received that strange telephone call. I am the one who believes but he had absolutely no explanation for it whatsoever.

I was just pleased that he'd had this experience as it has changed his outlook about spirit completely. We really believe that Bob had found a way of saying goodbye.

Julie, England

Sometimes the strangest thing about the sign is the interpretation. Is your experience an afterlife sign or simply a coincidence? You have to admit that they are slightly odd and really more like synchronicity (meaningful coincidences). Decide for yourself with this next true life story.

Personal Signs

When I was four years old I was given a beautiful black-and-white basset hound. We called him Pluto. He lived to the grand old age of fifteen and I was nineteen when he died. I'm now in my forties and, one day, I decided to have a bit of fun with the information I gained from one of your books. You suggested that it's OK to ask for a sign that a deceased loved one is around you; I asked for an image of my dog Pluto to be shown to me. Almost as soon as I did this I became cranky; I didn't actually have that many photos of him, and it wasn't as if the ones I had would suddenly fly out of my photo albums and land at my feet! I was disappointed at my request, believing I had wasted an opportunity for a sign.

A few days later I was wrapping up Xmas presents. The paper I was using had come from my late mother-in-law's house. When she passed away, the family found reams of wrapping paper which she had purchased but never used. Some of it was Xmas paper so I decided to put it to use. I was working quickly, worried that I might be disturbed by my children. I folded the paper over, tucked in the corners and was just about to put on the sticky tape when I looked down and saw that the paper I was using was covered with images of Walt Disney's cartoon dog Pluto! Hundreds of them! I just stood there staring at it in disbelief. I don't think I have ever before seen Xmas paper with Pluto on it and I knew straightaway it was my beautiful old friend bringing me the sign I had so longed for! Thanks, Pluto.

[*JACKY: Lesley had another strange 'coincidence' sign so I thought I'd share this one with you too.*]

My aunty passed away at a young age in 1996. We were both excellent tennis players and although I was nowhere near her standard, we both shared a great love of tennis. I decided to ask her to send me a tennis ball as a sign that she was OK and safe in heaven. The next day was Xmas Eve and my husband was leaving work early that night; in fact, I heard him pull into the driveway at lunchtime and I rushed out to meet him. He usually arrives home with arms laden with bags of work gear and often needs my help to carry it all in. Imagine my surprise when I opened the door and he was standing there holding nothing but a tennis ball! He casually explained that it had been lying on the side of the road as he was driving along so he stopped to pick it up. I was so taken aback that I didn't react straightaway, but later in the afternoon I explained to my husband about the sign I'd asked for. Funnily enough, he didn't think it was strange at all.

Lesley, Australia

Wasn't that an unusual sign? Although there are 'classic' signs, the best ones are those that have personal meaning for us . . . whatever the symbol turns out to be. Have you ever had an unusual sign from a loved one in the afterlife? Make sure you keep a special record of any experiences you might have had. Of course, I record my own personal experiences in the books I share with my readers but you might like to keep a little notebook with any unusual occurrences you have. Later you'll come to doubt what happened but it's easier to recall all the details if you have recorded them in some cherished way. It might be useful to share notes with other family members too; perhaps you can make a record of their afterlife signs as well?

Now, another story.

Safe in Heaven

My mother was a beautiful healthy woman of fifty-nine; a professional in the field of mental and physical disabilities. She was a talented artist, seamstress and a great friend.

Two days before my world fell apart I had the strangest dream. In the dream I was having coffee with my mam. Having drunk one cup she offered to make a fresh one and then said she would have to go. I was confused because I didn't think she was going out, but I remember saying, 'OK.' I remember seeing her making her way to the microwave and at that point I turned away. When I looked back she was gone. I searched for her all over the kitchen and she wasn't there. Then I focused on the patio doors to the garden and there in the garden was a beautiful oak coffin; it was shining in the sunlight and so lovely, but in a panic I awoke with my heart pounding.

The next morning I went to visit Mam and immediately told her of my strange dream. She smiled and said it was just a daft dream and not to worry, so I didn't. Then two days later my mam had a massive subarachnoid haemorrhage in the brain. Mam never regained consciousness and after the second day of hoping and praying that she would get well, I was aware of her speaking to me, inside my head. I was very tired and shrugged it off at first. Then it happened again, sweetly, softly, just as my mam spoke. She was telling me that I had to tell my twin sister that she had gone as she would never accept it from someone else.

I was heartbroken. Not only had my best friend gone, but I had the added responsibility of informing my sister.

I went to the toilets and cried. I didn't know what to do. I trusted what I was hearing and feeling but how could I tell my beautiful sister that our lovely mam had gone? After all, she was still warm, breathing on a ventilator and very much present. My mam's beautiful words stayed with me and I suddenly knew that I had to do it, it was my mam's last wish.

We'd been at the hospital for two days and we were very tired. I told my sister that I would take her for a coffee because we needed a break. Over coffee I swallowed hard and told her what had happened. I didn't know what to expect. I thought she might hate me for saying such things, but she looked into my teary eyes and as she welled up herself she said that she believed me. We held hands, hugged one another and returned to Mam's bedside.

We had only been back at the bedside for ten minutes or so when Mam took her final breath; she gave one big gasp against the ventilator, but we took great solace in knowing that we were there. Mam was pronounced brain-dead. My beautiful mam donated her organs. She was the most loving and giving person I have ever known.

One month later, with my sister and my children, I took a break in the Lake District. We were still grieving and, to be honest, it was a welcome distraction. One evening I couldn't sleep, I was lying on my right side and staring into the darkness wishing for sleep to come. Very suddenly I was aware of a pair of feet, bare apart from a pair of Scholl sandals. My heart jumped a little – Scholls were my mam's favourite shoe. At first I remember feeling a little bit scared. My eyes followed the feet upwards and I came face to face with my lovely mam. She had her hand across her lips to say *shh*, like it was a secret!

All of a sudden I was in a beautiful green park sitting on a bench. I was in awe of my surroundings because they were so gorgeous. The colours, the sounds of people laughing and chatting – even though I couldn't see anyone, I knew they were there. I turned to my right and there was my mam sitting right beside me. The first thing I remember saying was, 'But, Mam, you're dead!'

Then, inside my head, she said 'Yes, but look where I am . . . I am happy, please remember that . . . I love you and I always will.'

I don't remember crying because I was so stunned and so excited. I looked at her again and in a flash she was wearing every dress and outfit that I had remembered her wearing. It looked as if it was being projected on to her body for me to see. I felt so lucky and happy to be having this contact and suddenly I was back in my own bed. It was only then that the tears came. My beautiful mam had made sure that I knew she was well and I am certain she was thanking me for that difficult day in the hospital when I fulfilled her final wish.

The visit is as clear in my mind as the day it happened and one of my most memorable experiences.

Joanne, England

Isn't Joanne's story fantastic? By now I know you will have recognized several of the afterlife signs so that you are aware, as I am, that this was a spirit visitation experience and not a normal dream. Joanne was aware in the dream that her mother was dead so therefore she was lucid and aware during the encounter. 'Why are you here? You're dead, aren't you?' and other similar phrases are usually the point where the 'dream' turns into a 'visit' from a deceased loved one from the afterlife.

One of the reasons our loved ones come back from heaven is to clear up unfinished business. Over the years

I've heard stories of the deceased coming back to tell loved ones where they hid their will, for example, and even one who wanted to indicate to his sister who had killed him . . . a little scary, I think.

Saying sorry is common too. When we accept the apologies of the deceased it helps them to move on in their new life on the other side. Imagine when you pass over finding out that you were completely wrong about someone. That they had been accused of something . . . or worse, that YOU had accused them of something they hadn't done. That would weigh heavily on your conscience, wouldn't it? Visiting to apologize is helpful to both parties. You know that you'll forever feel cheated otherwise. 'They were wrong about me and I'll never be able to prove to them they were wrong now they are dead' is a burden no one wants to carry in life, so this type of contact is usually very welcome.

The lady in the next story wasn't accused of the 'crime' until after this man had passed over but it still turned her life upside down . . . she was innocent. The story is a little different to most of the rest of the stories in the book because the afterlife message comes through a psychic medium. It was so impressive and life-changing that I still wanted to use it here to illustrate the 'sorry' visitation phenomenon.

Saying Sorry

Having read two of your books, I felt compelled to write to you. I could relate to so many of the experiences that you'd written about. The experiences that pulled my attention the most were those where there was no question of doubt, where it defied all possibilities of it being a coincidence. The story I wish to share with you is just such a one. I need to tell you it all but as it is long and extended over many years I will try to condense it for you here.

During my first years of marriage (I married in 1968), I went to work for a company in a rather rough area of South-East London. I was the secretary to one of the managers and we worked very closely together. We became friends and sometimes spent our lunch breaks together. We were both going through marital problems at the time and so were able to talk to each other about what we were going through. It gave us both some comfort. At no time had our friendship become an affair; we were only ever just friends.

The company was due to move further south and the plan was that some of the staff would move with them. He was one of the people who had been chosen to move. By then I was pregnant with my first son so had left the company at the time the business was packing up to leave. After having my son I visited my friends and my boss to show them my son's photo; I was a proud mum. My boss (I will call him Terry) rushed into the office, said, 'Wow, you look great! Don't go away, I'll be back in a minute.' Then he returned with a beautiful bouquet for me, kissed me on the cheek and congratulated me. It was lovely.

The company duly packed up and left, and my husband and I moved to Kent where we were not on the telephone so contact between Terry and me was very rare until eventually we hardly ever communicated with each other. At the beginning of 1971 I was expecting my daughter and we went to visit my in-laws, who knew Terry. My husband and I both liked him very much so imagine our shock when my mother-in-law handed me a newspaper article reporting him as having killed his son, and then himself, after his marriage had broken down completely. It was a complete shock and so totally out of character.

He had left a letter saying that he'd been pushed over the edge by a woman who had pursued him constantly. The name was withheld but various things seemed to imply that it was me. I was traumatized. It was just ten weeks before the birth of my daughter when the police pushed into my house and accused me of sending threatening letters to his ex-wife, putting petrol through her letter box and many more horrific things that were not true. Our lives just fell apart. My husband and I went to the police station a few days before my daughter was born and we were told that they now had someone in custody (who had worked for the same company). The police wouldn't tell us who it was.

I had lived for so long feeling that someone hated me so much that they'd killed themselves and blamed me. Terry had died believing that I had been the culprit. I would never have done anything to hurt him, his family or anyone. It took me years to learn how to live with the thought that this friend had died believing it was me that had pushed him too far and I was left totally traumatized by the whole thing.

Unfortunately my own marriage eventually failed and many years later I moved to Berkshire where I lived with my youngest son and our resident ghost. We all confirmed it was a man and many people experienced his presence and tricks! We never knew who the ghost was. I have been a spiritual person since childhood and just accepted it as part of my life. Sometimes I would attend a spiritualist church but no one ever seemed to come through to me . . . I never had a psychic reading!

Then in 2003, whilst my daughter was living in London on the Kentish borders, I went to visit her one evening. She told me not to get settled because we were going to a spiritualist meeting as her friend had made a bet with her she would not go. My daughter was terrified, saying, 'Oh, what if they say something to me?' I was just plain excited, thinking about how much I enjoy hearing other people's happy stories relating to the afterlife.

What happened next, though, completely blew me away. After several readings the medium turned her attention to me. Did I know someone called Terry in the afterlife? I was astounded and could not answer for shock. She said that he wanted to tell me that he knew it wasn't me, and would I forgive him and accept these 'flowers'? She told me that even though he'd only ever bought me flowers once in his life, he wanted me to have these now. She was right; I just could not answer her because I was so blown away by the accuracy of her reading.

Then the psychic got very excited and begged me to answer him as she said that Terry wasn't telling her what the story was about but he was getting very upset about it and wanted me to accept the 'flowers'. I realized it was a sort of apology and was probably as important to him on his side of life as it was to me on my side.

At this point the medium walked over and stood next to me and asked what the problem was because, she said, 'Look what he is doing to me! Whatever is it?' As I looked at her, I could see her arms were covered in huge hives. Then the medium seemed to fade out from my vision and all I could see was Terry standing in front of me holding out his arms full of peace lilies (they are my favourite). I remember spluttering something like, 'Yes, of course, thank you . . .' Then I heard the medium speak again as Terry faded from view.

The medium explained that Terry was delighted and then dropped another bombshell: Terry had confessed to being my ghost . . . but in a good way. Apparently he was watching over me, especially when I slept. By this time my daughter had managed to slide under the chair in front of her because, of course, she knew nothing about what we had been talking about. When we got back to the car park and I explained to her, she cried and said, 'Oh, Mum!

How on earth have you lived with this for thirty-two years?' She was thrilled by my reading and asked me, 'How do you feel now?' I was so happy, I told her it was like being set free, especially to know that he was OK and happy again.

Now, in September 2011, I have had a dream visitation from him in which he had his son with him. They were both smiling and happy and it was wonderful to see him that way, especially knowing what he must have been through. I feel so blessed to have had these experiences, Jacky, and I felt I just had to share this with you.

Patricia, Egypt

I am delighted that Patricia shared her story with me here. Thirty-two years is a long time to wait for a visitation, but the way that Terry passed over, and the fact that he intentionally took another's life, would have meant extensive treatment and counselling of the soul on the other side of life. But more of this later.

A medium is involved in this next experience too, but only to confirm what this reader already knew. Life continues after death and Sonya's dad was going to prove it was true!

I Didn't Mean to Scare You!

My dad was seventy-eight years old and had been married for fifty-three years to my mum when he died suddenly of a heart attack on 2 July 2010. I had

95

always joked with him that I would find a way to contact him after he died and he would just smile politely because I don't think he believed in the afterlife. I was the one in the family that had always had an interest.

About two weeks after he died I woke up one night to find two figures standing next to my bed. I screamed in fright and then realized that one of the figures was Dad. Even though I couldn't see his face, I just felt it was him. Nothing was said or anything but I just felt peaceful, then I went back to sleep. In the morning I rang my mum and told her what had happened the night before. She was the only person I told.

About a week later I rang a medium whom I had never met before to make an appointment to ask about Dad. The first thing she said to me over the phone was that Dad was with her at that moment and that he said to say he was sorry, he hadn't meant to scare me the other night, he just wanted me to know he was OK, but I had woken up and screamed.

This took my breath away because no one but Mum knew about what had happened. I did have the appointment with the medium a few days later and some of the things she told me about Dad I didn't know (and this was useful for me to follow up as confirmation), but when I told Mum she knew exactly what the medium was talking about. The whole experience just blew me away and gave me a real belief that there is an afterlife.

Sonya, New Zealand

You can see the challenge that the deceased have when trying to visit us. They are not meant to scare us, yet even by accident it still happens sometimes. If you ask your loved one to visit you and let you know that they are OK, try not to be scared. That loving person you know in life is still a loving person in death. If your favourite aunt was adorable in life she isn't going to turn into a demonic figure once she reaches heaven-side, is she? OK, she's dead, I get your point . . . but she's still lovely!

Here is a misty visitation experience.

Saying Goodbye

I had a vivid dream where my gran came to see me (although she was still alive at the time). She entered through a wooden door into a room of clouds where I was waiting, and with her she had one of her sisters (there were six of them in her family). She told me that she had brought my great aunt to see me so that she could say goodbye. Although familiar, it was difficult to work out which sister it was because the vision I could see meant that she was quite like a vapour, but in human shape. We said our goodbyes, which were teary, and then they both left.

The next morning my mother called to say that my great auntie Kath had passed away (my gran's younger sister).

Flavia, England

It seems strange that Flavia's living gran appeared in the visitation experience but it's not as weird as you might think. I often get letters from readers who see me in their dream visitations. Apparently I usually appear either with angels, to talk about angels and the afterlife, or to support and guide them. Sadly, I have absolutely no recollection of doing this sort of work in my dreams at all! But I do believe them because so many readers have told me about it.

Our loved ones don't mean to scare us when they visit . . . that is why some stay away (in case you were wondering why your own loved ones hadn't popped over from heaven to say 'hi'.) Are you of a nervous disposition? If so, it might mean delays with your afterlife communication.

I can't say this often enough. The love we shared in life doesn't suddenly change when our deceased relatives and friends move to their new heavenly existence. Because many of these stopovers are so real, they can be frightening for the recipient – it challenges our reality. If our belief is that when we die we cease to exist, it can be a little mind-blowing when your dead uncle stops by in a dream to say goodbye! Yet millions of people around the world are having these encounters.

Having said that, as we have seen already, not all of these afterlife encounters happen in dreams; it's quite possible to be wide awake when a departed loved one pays a call. When faced with a manifestation of a spirit or the 'tricks' they seem to play (in a good way), you need to keep yourself calm even if it is someone you love very dearly! OK, I can hear you saying, it's all right for you, Jacky! But, I'll admit, even I get a little spooked out sometimes.

Right, let's enjoy another story.

Electrical Interference

I was introduced to your books by a friend who told me about a dream she had as a child, in which her grandfather, who was very poorly at the time – dying, in fact – visited her and how upset she felt afterwards. Being a small child, she didn't quite understand why she dreamt about her grandfather just before his death, and it was only when she read one of your books that she understood and accepted how special she was because her grandad had visited her to say goodbye.

I was fascinated by her story because I'd had similar experiences of my own. I shared them with my friend and ordered one of your books straight afterwards. I started reading your book and really enjoyed it. I was sitting on the sofa in my living room when suddenly my TV switched off; I thought there must have been a power cut but when I looked up I realized other devices and lights plugged through the same extension cable were all on. Also, the remote was on the other end of the sofa so I knew I couldn't have pressed the on/off button accidentally. The TV then switched itself back on a moment later.

It felt curious and funny rather than scary or alarming and so I carried on reading your book. It took me a couple of hours and getting through your book to a chapter dedicated to our loved ones who had passed over to realize it was the anniversary of my grandmother's death that very day; she must have come to remind me about it! Not for the first time as well. The same thing happened once on her death anniversary before. I told my friend who recommended your book to me about it and she was delighted with my story. Guess what I got from her for my birthday? Another one of your books!

A few years ago I was planning to light some candles at home on the day of my nan's death anniversary; when I was a child I remember her telling me that spirits were drawn to the light and that's why we light candles on the graves, so I wanted her to have her own light on that day. I came home from work and forgot about lighting candles though. I sat on the sofa and was reading or watching something when I heard a knock on the door. I went to open the door but there wasn't anyone there. I came back to sit down and heard another knock. Again, when I opened the door, there wasn't anyone there. It was only then I remembered it was Nan's 'special day' and thanked her for reminding me to light the candles for her!

Let me tell you a bit more about Nan and the rest of my family. Me, my mum, sister and Nan lived together up until Nan's death (though I do believe she still lives with all of us, or at least pops in for a visit every now and again!). When, as a child, I would tell my grandmother that I couldn't sleep because I was scared of ghosts, she would tell me, 'It's the living who can hurt you, not the dead, so you don't need to be afraid of them.' Maybe she was preparing me for her visits from the afterlife?!

On a few occasions I heard her talking in her sleep with her late brothers and sisters and she would often tell us about these dreams. It was her wish to die at home and that's where she passed away; peacefully, in her sleep, with her nearest and dearest there by her side, just as she wanted it.

A few months after Nan's death, me, my sister and Mum moved to a different flat in the same building. The first night in our new flat I dreamt about Nan coming down the stairs of the old flat we shared with her and heading towards the new one. My mum was so pleased when I told her about the dream, and we were all comforted by the thought that Nan had moved flats with us.

I carry a picture of my nan in my purse together with other family photographs. I hardly ever take them out; it's more about the comfort they give me having them with me at all times. One day I was home alone and going from the living room to the kitchen when I found Nan's picture, the one I keep in my purse, in the hall, by the front door. I know for a fact I didn't take it out of my purse; I know I didn't even take my purse out of my bag after coming back from work, so it must have been another one of Nan's visits!

If I may share another experience, a few days after my nan's funeral, a friend and neighbour told me how sorry she was about Nan's death but she thought it was lovely of Nan bringing her chocolates on the day she passed away. I was shocked to hear that because my nan was confined to bed in her last days of her life and wasn't able to do much for herself, so to learn she'd actually got out of bed, bought some chocolates (Where from? We lived on the third floor and for years Nan's legs were very weak and she wasn't able to leave the flat on her own) and gone to see my neighbour . . . ? Now, I've always thought that was my nan's spirit because it really would be extraordinary if she'd had the strength to do that a few hours before passing away! We felt it was Nan's way of saying goodbye to my friend and neighbour, possibly also making amends as they didn't always see eye to eye. If that's what it was, I think it was a lovely gesture on my nan's last day in this life!

After Nan's death my mum started collecting angel figurines and images. She must have hundreds of them now and all of our friends and family are always on the lookout for new angels for her. When I was reading your book I suddenly realized how many candles decorated with angels, figurines and ornaments I had in my flat. They are all gifts from family and friends. Then I realized I also had other angelic images too: pictures of cats and birds, hand-made fabric butterflies, bowls decorated with butterflies, hearts. I suddenly saw my flat in a very different, angelic light – full of love, light and hope.

Every time I discover a new angelic object I see it as a sign from my angels. It's like they're there for me and that they look after me, and I thank them for that and it makes me smile. Thank you for making me think about my special angelic friends and one very special relative indeed.

Aggie, England

It's not just everyday folk that have these heavenly experiences. I thought you might like to read the next section . . . just for fun.

Experiences of People in the Public Eye

Many well-known names have had experiences too; the list includes Winston Churchill, Pope John Paul II, Abraham Lincoln, Benjamin Franklin, Mark Twain, Robert Louis Stevenson, Carl Jung and Henry Ford! Stars from stage and screen have also had afterlife contact and many have been happy to discuss their experiences with the public. It's no longer embarrassing to share one's paranormal encounters it seems – thank goodness!

Pope John Paul II

Hit by a gunshot, an assassination attempt, as he entered St Peter's Square to address an audience on 13 May 1981, the Pope was critically wounded. Pope John Paul, the leader of the Roman Catholic Church, was lying close to death and floating in and out of consciousness. Afterwards the Pope discussed how difficult the experience had been, but talked about being 'practically on the other side', as doctors gave him life-saving blood. The Pope had lost nearly three-quarters of his blood and went through five hours of surgery. Afterwards he reported that he felt Our Lady Fatima had been with him during the ordeal: 'I felt that extraordinary motherly protection and care, which turned out to be stronger than the deadly bullet,' he recalled.

> 'Have no fear of moving into the unknown.
> Simply step out fearlessly knowing that
> I am with you, therefore no harm can
> befall you; all is very, very well. Do this in
> complete faith and confidence.'
>
> Pope John Paul II

He survived until 2005, finally passing away on 2 April following a urinary tract infection. His final words translate as 'Let me depart to the house of the Father.' He was ready to go 'home' to heaven.

Robert Louis Stevenson

The author regularly had spiritual types of ethereal experiences and learnt how to put himself into trance-like states. That day-dream half-awake/half-asleep condition, or hypnagogic state, can be self-created with practice. Stevenson taught himself how to do this and regularly strapped himself into a type of harness. As he fell asleep, the harness would nudge him awake; performing this trick over and over again, it would keep him aware during this trance state and helped him to write his novels by almost 'channelling' the information from other realms and gathering ideas for his books during trances and dreams. His work very much reflects his other-worldly real-life experiences.

Carl Jung

The world-renowned psychiatrist had a heart attack, followed by a near-death experience, whilst in hospital in Switzerland in 1944. He found himself high up above the earth, which he saw bathed in a wonderful blue light. He describes the sea and continents and picked out various countries, including the reddish-yellow desert of Arabia and the snow-covered Himalayas.

He described his experience as looking at a map. It was only later that he understood he would need to have been a thousand miles from earth to have been able to see the sight he saw whilst floating in space!

> 'As far as we can discern, the sole purpose of human existence is to kindle a light in the darkness of mere being.'
>
> Carl Jung

In his new 'state of death' he felt he now carried with him everything he had ever been or done . . . he was his own history. [*Jacky: Rather like the near-death review we discussed in an earlier chapter?*]

Just as he was about to discover more, to become aware of why he existed, his purpose in life and how he fitted into everything there was, he was called back to his body by an avatar-type figure which was to him the embodiment of his doctor. There had been a 'protest', he said, against him leaving the earth and he had to return. [*JACKY: Because it wasn't 'his time'?*]

This news was of great disappointment to him; life in a human body seemed almost like a prison to him now he was floating freely in his spiritual body! More worryingly, Jung was concerned that his own doctor might be near death himself to have appeared to him in this way. Bizarrely, Jung turned out to be the doctor's last patient as the doctor himself died of septicaemia a short while later! So the doctor really was near death, exactly as Jung had seen.

Queen Elizabeth I

Elizabeth had a near-death experience when she contracted smallpox in October 1562, and although I could find no recorded 'experience', she seems to have had some kind of precognition during her lifetime. No one could say she was not intuitive during her leadership and extraordinary reign.

The Queen was said to have always had a 'strange feeling' about her Coronation ring, believing that if it was ever removed, she would die. It was one of her most prized possessions and she wore it constantly for the whole forty-five years of her reign. By 1603, the ring had grown into her flesh and her advisers insisted it be removed. A week later she died, so maybe she had been right after all! In her final days she sat with the Archbishop of Canterbury. The Queen clung tightly to his hand and as he spoke to her about of the joys of heaven, she is said to have squeezed his hand contentedly.

Elizabeth herself now visits from the other side. Her ghost is to be found in many places nowadays; apparently she even haunts the royal library at Windsor Castle in Berkshire. The late princess Margaret, sister to Queen Elizabeth II, personally saw the ghost of Queen Elizabeth I in the library and, on another occasion, a guard officer followed the former Queen into the library, whereupon she suddenly disappeared. Supposedly she also makes an annual appearance in the courtyard of Richmond Palace every 24 March, the anniversary of her death in 1603 at the age of sixty-nine. If you're interested, perhaps you could check it out!

Mark Twain

Real name Samuel Langhorne Clemens, author Mark Twain is said to have experienced three separate near-death experiences, although material to substantiate this has been challenging to discover. He also had psychic experiences throughout his life. Whilst training to be a steamboat pilot, Samuel convinced his younger brother Henry to join him. Tragically, Henry was killed when the *Pennsylvania*, the steamboat he was working on at the time, exploded. Curiously, Twain had had a dream a month earlier which predicted the death. The premonition inspired his interest in parapsychology (study of the psychic) and he became one of the founding members of the Society for Psychical Research.

> 'The reports of my death are greatly
> exaggerated.'
>
> Mark Twain

Sadly, much of Twain's life was surrounded by death. He was the sixth child of seven but only three survived childhood. His father died of pneumonia when Twain was just eleven years old and he lost three of his own four children and his wife before his own passing.

Twain was born within two weeks of the closest approach to earth of Halley's Comet. Many years later he seemed also to predict his own death and is quoted as saying, 'I came in with Halley's Comet in 1835. It is coming again next year, and I expect to go out with it. It will be the greatest disappointment of my life if I don't go out with Halley's Comet. The Almighty has said, no doubt: "Now here are these two unaccountable freaks; they came in together, they must go out together."' His prediction was true and he passed away on 21 April 1910, one day after Halley's Comet's closest approach to earth.

After his death his daughter Clara is reported as saying: 'Sometimes he believed death ended everything, but most of the time he felt sure of a life beyond.'

'I do not fear death. I had been dead
for billions and billions of years before
I was born, and had not suffered the
slightest inconvenience from it.'

Mark Twain

I always believe that the next best thing to having an after-life experience is probably to read about them. My hope is that you don't just find these stories a curiosity but that you find comfort in them too. Let's go and explore the subject a little more.

More Messages From Heaven

'Be at peace with your own soul, then
heaven and earth will be at peace with you.'
St Jerome

Receiving personal communication from the afterlife is always going to be the best way of 'proving' that heaven is a real place where we live on after our earthly lives have finished. So many people are having these types of experiences now, it's more common than uncommon – no longer a paranormal experience and more of a normal one. I know it's hard when these things haven't happened to you but often when people read my books they recall an experience that they'd buried away, maybe because they weren't ready to acknowledge that the experience had been real. 'Oh yes,' they'll tell me, 'years ago I had something just like that happen to me.' So it's possible that you've hidden your encounter even from yourself and maybe with good reason. We protect ourselves from things that our minds can't handle.

When you read that some people are at first frightened (if not terrified) by their afterlife communication, then you know why you might have tucked away your own experience at the back of your mind, waiting until you were ready to assimilate the experience into your waking life. Reading about others' heavenly encounters can be the catalyst to either recalling your previous contact or to prompting a new visitation.

I do a lot of radio 'phone-ins' where callers will ring the station with their personal experiences and questions. I love doing this but I am always sad when people call in to explain how they are grieving and tell me how much they would love an experience but haven't had one . . . yet. These dream visitations, real visits from the other side, are the most powerful type of communication there is, but don't forget that our loved ones reach out to us in many ways, including bringing us white feathers as signs that they are around, ringing bells, setting off alarms and numerous other signals that they are with us and love us still.

There is a universal law of 'non-interference' – just like on the *Star Trek* television show and movies – non-interference in our world by beings from outside our world and of us on other worlds. Beings from outside of the planet are not permitted to interfere or influence our free will. Incidentally, fans believe that *Star Trek* creator Gene Roddenberry (Eugene Wesley Roddenberry) created the series based on the idea of preparing the public for future visits from beings from outer space (he was requested to write the series for television).

Roddenberry did believe in paranormal phenomena and one wonders where his storylines came from in the first place! Records indicate that Roddenberry had an out-of-body experience as a child, and we know that many (including myself) who've had either near-death or out-of-body experiences seem to go on to have other paranormal phenomena happen throughout their lives. He also sometimes referred to something he called the 'All', or the life force of the Universe; which he occasionally explained as 'God'. Excuse this little diversion here but I think it's important to point out how Roddenberry (along with other writers) has influenced the way we think about life outside of our planet, especially noting how popular the *Star Trek* series has been throughout the world. And even though we are talking about alien worlds and visitors, it's hard to know where one topic ends and the next (the afterlife) might begin!

If we look back at the list on the previous page where I have indicated the different ways that the departed can interact with us, it means that they, our spirit friends, can soothe and comfort us but not frighten us or make our grieving worse. It's a fine line between the two. Inevitably, a visit from the other side will mean that you may initially miss the person more than ever. What if their visit frightens you? This does happen, as we know, despite the best of intentions. When we worry about being frightened by a visit it can also stop it happening . . . I think this is where reading stories of other people's encounters can help. Once you understand how it works, the fear, for the most part, seems to go away, and contact is allowed to happen. Let's look at another experience.

It Felt so Real

My mam died when I was only ten years old and not a day goes by that I don't think of her. However, I was always scared in case she appeared in front of me, which I knew would 'freak me out'. At the age of thirty I started reading about angels and the after-life and I was particularly interested in how I could ask my mam to use more subtle ways to show me that she was around.

A few months later I had a very realistic dream. I was lying in bed when my deceased grandmother came into my room. She told me she had brought my mam with her and that I should not be scared. She told me that Mam was going to give me a hug and she did. It was so real I actually felt the sensation of this happening; I could feel her arms around me. I knew I was asleep at the time (my body was asleep), but this felt so real. The hug lasted only a minute and then I woke up. Strangely, I could still feel the hug for days afterwards as if she continued to stay close to me. Mam hasn't visited or left any signs since, although I continue to ask her to do so.

Paula, Co. Durham

I love Paula's story but it does highlight another issue: once we've had an experience, we want more . . . and more. I've had loads of afterlife contact from my own deceased loved ones but it never seems to be enough for me either. I think it's important to note that although we gain reassurance from contact with our deceased loved ones, it doesn't mean we stop missing them on this side of life.

Here is another story, this time from Karen who was left a young widow with two sons.

Well Now

My sons, Kieran and Sean, were sleeping with me in my bed one night. They were only twelve when their dad died. David appeared to me one night and I actually woke Sean up and said, 'I've just seen Dad.' Sean looked at me as if I had finally 'lost it' completely. This is what happened . . .

I was suddenly standing in front of David. I could see a pale blue colour around me but couldn't make out any shapes. He clearly spoke to me and I physically felt him hold my hands in his. He said to me, 'George will be here soon . . .' which is true, his older brother had died a month after him but his funeral had not taken place at that time.

Then he said, 'My mum is just over there . . .' but I couldn't see her. David suffered from really bad arthritis and walked with crutches during his life. He told me he didn't need his crutches any more and he didn't have them in heaven. I told him I wanted to stay with him in heaven but he said to me, 'You can't, you need to go now.' I think the dream visitation was him saying goodbye because he'd died so suddenly.

The next thing I remember is waking Sean to tell him about the experience and I still remember every detail even to this day. I felt a heat in my hands the next day still and I know that he really did hold my hands. Maybe I wasn't meant to see anything else but

I'm sure it was heaven that I went to. It remains and always will be a treasured and wonderful memory.

Karen, Scotland

This next story also includes the feeling of heavenly touch . . . and a little something extra magical. Perhaps timing is everything, as this experience shows.

Stars

I had contacts from my own lovely dad who died in February 2000. A few days after he died, I was sorting the washing out when I felt a gentle but firm rub on my cheek. It was as if someone had stroked it. I feel it was Dad trying to reassure me because I was so sad and shocked when he left us. [*JACKY: If we're awake when a visitation happens we tend to be either very relaxed or in a daydream-like state of mind, the sort you fall into when doing boring tasks like washing up or ironing . . . or in this case, sorting the washing. Something you could do without having to think too much about it. This leaves the mind free to wander and explore and the deceased to reach out to us.*]

Dad was seventy-nine when he died. He hadn't been well, but had not been expected to die. The visit from him was so lovely.

That night I felt unable to get to sleep and kept watching the stars out of a bedroom window. I immediately thought of Dad again and said, 'Dad, please send me a shooting star to tell me you're OK.' And a second or two later I watched as a shooting star shot across the sky! It was a very special moment indeed.

Ann (location withheld)

What it does do is help us to accept the reality. It's as if our lost relations are still alive; imagine maybe they are on some extended holiday in a location far, far away and that one day, once we've saved up enough money (i.e., it's 'our time'), then we can join them in their luxury accommodation at their exotic destination. Of course, leaving the earth plane means leaving everything we love about this side of life behind too, so don't wish it away too quickly! Our loved ones certainly don't want us to join them (hence the reason they are always pushing us back and telling us it's not 'our time'!).

Think instead of what you can do to honour them on this side of life. What can you do to make them proud of you? Let the loss help you to achieve your own life goals rather than stop you from moving forward.

Over and over again the deceased have told the living, 'It's not your time,' and 'Go back, you have work to do!' Just as in heaven, we have things we need to accomplish on this side of life. It's important to explore your world, try new things and help others. How much better it would be to arrive at the pearly gates and say, 'Boy, what a ride that was! My life was a blast – I loved it all: the good, the bad . . . I learnt from every experience.' I can imagine nothing more heartbreaking than getting to the end of my life and realizing, 'Oh dear, I've just wasted my life away!' Tragic.

Love Means They Can Find Us Anywhere

Many people worry that their deceased relatives will not find them if they move house or go on holiday, but the following dream visitation shows how this is not the case. Our loved ones are drawn to our energy essence (like that magnet again?) rather than a familiar location or somewhere they knew on earth. It's possible they may use our moving house as an opportunity not to visit so often, but only if this were going to happen at some point anyway. There is always a natural end or slowing down to the visits; it's as if they are saying, 'I've come to let you know I am OK but now I must continue my new life and you must carry on with yours.'

Here is Aoife's story.

On Holiday

After Mom passed away I had a dream that I was on the phone to her and she said she was in heaven. Mom told me that she was going to see my grandmother, her mom, later on.

While I was in Spain on holiday I had another dream. This time I was in the swimming pool and, as I got out, I saw a woman who looked very much like my mom. She was on a chair sunbathing and wearing sunglasses (which my mom used to wear a lot!). I stared at her and then she sat up and said to me, 'Are you OK?' I apologized for staring at her and replied, 'You look like my mother.'

The woman took off the sunglasses and said, 'That's because it's me, I'm here with you in Spain.' She explained, 'You might not be able to see me, but I'm here all the time.' Then she gave me a big hug and I can't explain how real it felt. I woke up feeling so good that morning, those words were so reassuring. I think Mom comes to me in dreams because she knows I won't be afraid. [*JACKY: I hear this message a lot. Our loved ones are often sitting with us at family occasions, joining in, although no one is aware of them. Those moments when you think, 'I wish Mum/Dad/Aunty/my brother/my friend etc. could be with us today,' that is when they probably are with you. You have picked up on their presence just as they intended.*]

In another dream I was with my two brothers, sister, Dad and my mom's brother; we were away in the country. In the dream we were all sitting down at a table, talking and laughing with one another, and my mom was at the table but no one could see her or hear her but me. She would listen to the stories and laugh along with everyone else, as if she was alive and really taking part!

I don't think a week goes by where I don't see her in a dream; sometimes randomly she will appear and just give me one of her motherly warm hugs, and it will feel amazing. I feel honoured that I have these dreams because it makes me excited to go to sleep so I can see my mom and talk to her.

Aoife, Ireland

My dad appeared in a dream a little like this. The family were all sitting down in a small room with lots of comfortable chairs. We were chatting and having fun. Then I happened to glance up and realized that Dad was occupying one of the chairs. Immediately I became lucid and aware and asked him, 'Dad, what are you doing here?' He realized he'd been spotted and stood up to go. He just grinned at me and he faded away. He too was showing me, 'I am often part of family gatherings. Don't think for one minute that just because you can't see me it doesn't mean I am not here!'

Like many of these experiences, the 'dream space' where we were sitting seemed to be created in the lower heavenly realms ... almost as if the cosy sitting-room space had been created for us all to get together in the astral realms. It was an opportunity for us to visit. It's a theme that pops up over and over again.

Getting Our Attention

Subtle experiences as signs from the other side can be comforting but, let me warn you, if you ask for something a little more dramatic you'd better be sure this is what you want! If you suddenly hear the sound of 'someone' washing up in the kitchen accompanied by the crashing of pots and pans you might not like it as much as you'd thought you would.

Our loved ones sometimes have the ability to make items appear and disappear. You might walk out of the room thinking of your late husband and walk back into the room moments later to see a necklace (maybe one he bought you on your anniversary) lying on the bed. When there is no one else in the room, how else do you explain this phenomenon apart from saying that it's a gift from heaven?

Here is Sue's story:

Book Story

My dad died of cancer in April 2004. I had always believed in the afterlife, but my dad didn't; I thought there was no way he would ever come through with a message if I went to see a psychic medium.

Two weeks after he died we left Mum's and headed for home. It was the day of the funeral and I was feeling desperately sad sitting in the front room on my own. Just then I heard an almighty thud, I looked up and a photo of my children, which had been hanging on the wall, had thrown itself off the wall and on to the floor! The funny thing was that it was the same photo that I'd put into Dad's coffin when we went to see him at the chapel of rest, so it seemed like a pretty clear sign.

I went over to the wall to investigate and the photo would have needed to have been lifted up into the air before it would have come off the picture hook. The photograph had been securely hung on a large hook, and the hook was still in place. It left me wondering but I just hung the picture back on the wall and forgot about it.

Later that evening we all went to bed; I lay awake for a while but it felt like something was around me. I had the sensation of my hair being tickled, but eventually I fell asleep. About 3.00 a.m. I was woken by the sound of a loud crashing downstairs. I thought we had burglars, so at first I was reluctant to go and find out what it was. Then it went quiet and I felt brave enough to tiptoe down the stairs. I was stunned at what I saw. All of the books from the bookshelf under the stairs were all over the hall floor. They must have been thrown off the shelf because we have a desk under the bookshelf and if the bookshelf had tipped somehow, the books would have fallen on to the desk. Some of the books were quite a distance from the desk and they were all up the hallway. As I stood watching I got the feeling that someone was tickling my head again! Dad?

Since that time we've had a few more photographs fall from the wall . . . it seems to be Dad's party trick; but since I have been to a medium and had a message from my dad, these things don't occur as often. It seems that it was Dad's initial need to contact us and let us know that he had 'survived' that he urgently wanted to communicate and this was one way he was able to do this.

We do still get contact from time to time, usually if my dad is trying to tell me that my mum needs help. Whenever I see something fall off a shelf or a photo come off a wall it's because Mum isn't well or something has gone wrong at her house. It seems strange that Dad didn't believe in the afterlife but I know he does now.

Sue, England

My own deceased relatives, though they love to ring door-bells, never knock on the door; some spirits, however, certainly prefer this method!

Knock, Knock . . . Who's There?

When I was a kid my grandfather always said that when he died he'd knock on my front door. This became one of his jokes, for years he would talk about it. When he passed there was often a knock at the door and no one was there. I know this was him and it was funny as I'm sure he still treated it as a joke even from the other side.

Anthony, England

Piggybacking Others' Afterlife Experiences

As I mentioned earlier, back in 2011 my sister Madeline Richardson and I wrote a book called *Call Me When You Get to Heaven*. It charted our family experiences relating to our dad Ron's passing. Dad promised he would help me write a book when his time finally came, and from the moment he passed over he began to communicate with his family. Dad visited each of his four daughters in dreams on the first night he passed on and the experiences were shared with around twenty family members and friends who each in turn had their own spirit visits from Dad. We even appeared on Channel 5's *Live with Gabby Logan* show, as well as SKY TV, and in various magazines and national newspapers, so even more people were able to share our encounters with the afterlife.

It's important to note here that I became interested in the afterlife *because* of the experiences my family and I had had for many years, rather than the experiences coming *after* I started writing. But for many others, it works the other way round. I was so excited by the afterlife contact I'd received personally (an old school friend first, then many years later my uncle, an assortment of other friends and relatives, my dad and lastly my mum's sister, my aunt.).

My own encounters with the other side were fascinating to me . . . I wondered if others might enjoy reading about them. I found my afterlife contact to be immediately comforting. If our loved ones can reach out to us post-mortem then it becomes apparent that they don't die . . . not in the way we understand death. Our consciousness, the personality part of our mind that makes us 'us', seemed to live on. This was the most exciting discovery of my life and right away I felt that this was also my life mission – my existence, my reason for being here on earth right now was to share this discovery with others so that they too might be comforted by it!

The exciting thing is that once people had read our book about Dad, many of our readers began to have their own experiences; it was as if their own loved ones were piggybacking our story. This has happened before: when people have read my books (or books written by others) about this afterlife phenomenon they begin to think about their own passed-over loved ones. Thinking about the deceased seems to prompt visitation experiences, so many people wrote to share their own stories of what happened to them after Dad passed on. Maybe our readers felt more confident at the thought of contact once they had a better understanding of the phenomenon?

Our story is an emotional one and was written throughout the grieving process. The story, like life itself, is full of laughter and tears. One family friend was reading the book in the bath when the towel on the rail slipped to the floor. She burst out laughing and said out loud, 'Is that you, "Uncle Ron"? You shouldn't be in here, I am in the bath!' Coincidence? Yes, if you like, but at the time she was feeling a little sad at his loss. Towels do slip from the towel rail but what followed next was a little harder to explain. Reading more of the book in bed later that night, a jacket – which had been hanging on a hook behind my friend's bedroom door for many months – suddenly fell to the floor too. She explained to me that for it to have done this, it would have needed to have been lifted up from the hook ... Now, these things don't happen on their own – do they? No! As we've already seen, our spirit friends seem perfectly capable of lifting thing up from hooks and nails!

Needless to say, my friend found the whole thing hysterical ... and also comforting. She explained that on each occasion she'd reached a particularly sad part of the book so the timing was perfect! I noticed the similarity between this story and the picture hook in the story earlier. In both cases these spirits have had to manipulate something on our side of life to create the phenomenon.

I received several emails from fans who had had visits from heaven after they'd read our book. This was one of my favourites.

Just Like Your *Dad*

I have read your book *Call Me When You Get to Heaven*, and would like to tell you of the incredible similarities between your story and mine. My dad passed away on 8 November 2011 and afterwards my husband bought me your book.

Dad lived in West Sussex and had suffered from chronic emphysema for just over five years. Although distance separated us, we telephoned Dad every morning and evening. Much of 2011 was spent travelling to Dad's home; he was being cared for in a care home in East Wittering. Like your dad, my dad was also a Ronald, known by everyone as Ron. His nickname, like your dad, was 'Rocket Ron' and he too loved fishing and had an Uncle Erne.

On 7 November last year I received a telephone call to tell me that Dad was failing fast. Once we arrived I spent several hours talking to Dad and I know that he could hear me because he smiled and turned his head towards me a number of times. In the early hours I held his hand and said to him, 'Dad, for my own selfish reasons I would love to keep you here but you're tired and you have suffered enough; it's time to let go, Mum is waiting for you.' I told him that I loved him with all my heart, and twenty minutes later he passed away.

Days later I was still very upset and my husband took me out in the car for some fresh air. I just wanted to speak to my dad one last time. Later in the evening when I was reading your book I turned to the start of the chapter entitled 'Visiting Hours' and found a white feather wedged in the spine. Then on another day I found a pristine white feather wedged in with the flowers at work.

Some time later a friend asked me if I'd found any more feathers. I said, 'No, I think Dad's forgotten about me.'

Unusually that day at work I was asked to help out by working one of the tills and as soon as I opened the cash drawer I discovered another white feather. I just knew that it was Dad letting me know that he had not forgotten me after all.

Linda, Scotland

Isn't that story fun? White feathers are such a simple sign that our loved ones are OK in heaven; those feathers turn up in the most unusual of places. I've seen them every day since I've been working on this book. Yesterday one floated right across the car windscreen and the day before that I had one fall at my feet. Fabulous! I love to think of it as a sign that I am being assisted from the other side. You don't think I write these books on my own, do you?

Heaven on Earth?

Sometimes I wonder if we forget that earth can occasionally be like 'a little piece of heaven' too. Feeling a bit down recently, my husband, John, suggested we both go for a walk on a nearby beach. Gwithian beach in Cornwall is miles of golden, uninterrupted sand but as we arrived the wind was blowing so strongly I almost changed my mind. Wearing a scarf round my head, a hat and a hood, along with sunglasses to protect my eyes, we walked down the cliff steps and on to the sand. The sand was blowing across the beach like a sandstorm in the desert but it was surprisingly beautiful. The cliffs were actually protecting most of the beach from the high winds and our walk was simply breathtaking as the waves crashed up on to the shore. Almost immediately the sun began to shine. At the other end of the beach, a perfect rainbow emerged from the light cloudy sky. It arched artistically over the top of the lighthouse and John managed to capture the rainbow on his mobile phone.

After walking back up to the car we sat drinking out of a flask and looking out over the sea below. Moments later a group of wild ponies appeared and I jumped back out of the car to take a photograph on my mobile phone . . . Taking photographs is such a fantastic way of zoning in on an object of beauty – it really makes you concentrate on the picture before you.

Feeling rather magical, we drove back to town to pick up some supplies. Walking along the high street I could hear a lot of splashing water and looked up. A blackbird was taking a bath in a length of drainpipe running along the top of one of the buildings. I walked all the way to the car with a big smile on my face. What an uplifting day!

When I finally depart earth for heaven I hope I remember special moments like this. I know it's a cliché but a newborn baby, spring flowers or even a sunset – these are moments to treasure. Sadly, following the loss of a close relation, some people become so frightened of dying themselves that they forget to LIVE. This is a regular message from folk on the other side of life. They remind us, 'I know I have died but I want you to carry on. Enjoy your life . . . I'll be waiting for you in the future but, for now, make the most of every single moment.' We really must.

Still Watching Over Us

Sometimes our dream visitations are purely to let us know that our loved ones are aware of what is going on in our current lives. It's not that our loved ones have any urgent messages from heaven but that they just want us to know about our 'happy endings'.

The deceased are still interested in what happens in our lives, they still love us, they still care about us. We finally got pregnant; we met someone and fell in love; we eventually passed our driving test . . . don't worry, your loved one likely knows this, even though they are no longer in a body. Here is Pam's story.

Still a Grandma in Heaven

I had a dream visitation and I wanted to share it with you. In this dream I was driving to meet my late mum 'in the country'. She was waiting for me in a pub car park but it was surrounded by lots of lovely lush green trees, grass and beautiful flowers. The sun was shining brightly; it was a beautiful scene! [*JACKY: Sound familiar, dear reader?*]

As I approached my mum she was sitting peacefully on a wooden bench. She looked younger in age, about in her thirties; the prime of her life. I sat down beside her and we gazed at each other peacefully and we held hands. I told her that I'd missed her and she replied that she knew – that she was aware of my feelings. It was like she knew my thoughts about her in the physical world. We sat for a few moments just holding hands and looking at each other. I felt this overwhelming pure divine love coming from her . . . it was amazing. She seemed to be showing me that even though she was not with me in the physical world any more, the strong love that connected us was still there between the two different worlds.

My mum then said, 'I've come to tell you something. Andy [my brother, whom I love very much] will get married in September and will have his own home.' My brother had been in a long-distance relationship which my mum was aware of before her passing, and we had spoken together of my brother finding true happiness with someone special. I took the information and just smiled. Then my mum said, 'It's time for you to go now.' I kissed my beautiful mum, walked back to my car and drove off leaving her where she was, looking contented.

The baby girl, Mum's granddaughter, is my brother and his partner's. But before the baby was born my brother told me he had a dream from our beautiful mum too. They were in a garden and held hands facing each other, and together they walked around the garden. My brother was woken from the dream with a phone call from his long-distance partner to say that she had gone into labour! Perhaps Mum knew? Their little baby girl was born on 14 October. Mum would have been delighted . . . but, of course, she already knows all about it.

Mum and I had discussions about how she wanted my brother to find true happiness with someone special and have a family of his own one day. After she passed on it happened and I felt sad that my mum wasn't present to see it for herself. I had been thinking a lot about this: not only had my mum now got a beautiful granddaughter but she also had a grandson too. So there were two grandchildren whom she would have adored. It was just so sad.

One night I went to bed and had a profound vision; it was as clear as anything. Mum was standing in perfect health holding both babies in her arms; she had a warm smile and was so happy! I wondered if Mum had visited to reassure me that she was aware of her grandchildren on earth even though she was in the spirit world. I also felt the love she had for them and sensed that she will always be with them to guide them through their life, like a guardian angel. So, after all, all my worries came to nothing: Mum was a grandma just as well in heaven as she could have been on earth.

Although I have not discussed the dream I had with Mum about my brother getting married, I'm sure it will come true. I can't wait!

Pam, England

Heavenly Attire

What do the deceased wear in heaven? I cover this in the Q&A chapter towards the end of the book but, briefly, the answer is *whatever they want*. As spirit they are beings of light but when they visit the earth plane they appear in the body of their recently deceased human bodies and wear something they love ... or we love. Items of clothing have included:

- The clothes they were buried in (especially if those items were distinctive) – useful if you were

131

unaware of what they were buried in as it acts as proof that the visit was a real one.
- The sort of thing you recognize them in: uniform, biker gear, bright colours, funky jewellery, hats and so on.
- Something that you may have bought them.
- Something they are wearing in a photograph of them that you love.
- Something they would have worn on earth had they only been slim enough, the right shape, etc.
- An ethereal gown to show you their new lighter status as a spirit of light.

What Do They Look Like in Heaven?

Again, they can appear to us any way they wish. When first passing over they retain their earthly shape. Illnesses fade away or are healed (there is no need for the soul to maintain their earthly sickness and in time this is 'healed'). Souls usually appear as their best possible selves; they have the long hair they always wanted, or used to have, they choose to appear or look as young healthy adults – old enough to show wisdom, young enough that they don't have wrinkles!

As they evolve and settle into their heavenly home many just assume their soul forms once more. They appear glowing, like twinkly clouds of light. Other souls easily recognize each other and have no need of the earthly visual representations.

In dream visitations souls may visit the living in this way but normally they choose an earthly form. Different people will see the deceased in different ways. Grandchildren may see their grandparents much as they looked on earth (complete with false teeth, walking sticks, etc.), then over time they will lose these earthly things.

Souls who passed as young children will often appear to their parents at the age in which they passed on. Of course, their bodies were young but it doesn't mean the soul was. If they appear several times over the years they appear to 'grow up' at the rate their brothers and sisters do.

Whatever age your loved one appears, you'll probably recognize them. There is a soul connection, a deep knowing that binds us together. We are connected in heaven as we were on earth and the connection to the departed stays the same.

Caz is a Facebook friend and she was kind enough to share her story.

Dad Looks Great

Dad died in 1998, and a few weeks after his funeral he visited me in a dream. It was so real that I wanted to hug him but I couldn't move! He was dressed in clothes I could remember him wearing and he looked really smart; his white hair looked shiny and soft and he looked so well and healthy. [*JACKY: And we know why she couldn't touch him, don't we!*]

I almost cried as I was so pleased to see him. He was sitting on top of his grave with his legs straight out in front of him yet it seemed to me that he was hovering over the top of the grave. Dad looked at me, smiled and said, 'There's no need to worry about me now, I'm fine.' Then he disappeared before I could reply, but I felt so at peace afterwards it was amazing.

I've never forgotten it and I can still see him now as clear as he was then; I'm convinced that he visited me to reassure me that he was still with me.

Do They Live in Houses in Heaven?

In the lower 'entrance' levels of heaven, the waiting and meeting areas, there are buildings and resting areas – although, strictly speaking, as spirits don't need to rest, sleep or eat, houses aren't really necessary. Buildings are mainly shown as places to learn, play and socialize. There are also 'buildings' for other things like healing, orientation and gathering with one's soul groups (other souls we share different roles with over many different lifetimes).

We can have homes if we wish to, but as before, once we develop spiritually we grow out of the need for such places, knowing they are unnecessary. Spiritual beings of light don't need houses made of bricks, wood or straw!

Some souls who visit heaven, either through near-death experience or dream-type visitations, do sometimes see buildings.

- Many report seeing 'Halls of Learning', like giant libraries, which appear as rooms full of books (you don't need to read the books in the usual way, you sort of absorb the information from them). The information is shown as interactive pictures that you can view or take part in (like the 'life reviews' you read about earlier in the book).

- Cities made of precious stones and crystals.
- Buildings made of beautiful colours (some not known from earth, or which our human eyes cannot perceive).
- Religious buildings; those who wish to continue with their earthly religions may gather here at first.
- Smooth marble-type surfaces on walls.
- Carved, artistic structures of 'classical' appearance (including statues and columns).

The realms of spirit are not static in the way that things are on earth and can be manifested and dematerialized if the need arises.

Time and Space

When Dad came to visit me after he passed on he showed me things that were going to happen in the future . . . my earthly future timeline. At first it was difficult to understand what he was showing me (and my sisters, who experienced similar phenomena), but later, as his visions manifested in reality, our reality, it became clearer what he had been showing us.

Time as we measure it on earth does not seem to exist in the heavenly realms. If your loved ones take moments or years to visit you, to them it seems as if no time has passed at all. It's difficult for us to understand how time cannot exist – we live a linear life with a past, present and future timeline. We look back at things that have happened to us and forward to experiences planned. We live by the clock and work by our calendars. Without them it would be difficult to plan – our lives would seem chaotic – yet because I work from home, the need for clock and calendars is mostly extinct. I have several pretty watches but wear them as pieces of jewellery only when I go out. I can't usually read the time without my glasses on anyway and I work when the mood takes me.

I keep strange hours (by others' standards), and only need to know the day and date if I have been asked to appear on TV, speak on the radio, give a book-signing or attend a speaking engagement. Luckily for me, my husband acts as my clock and calendar keeper. He even signals me when I am onstage to indicate when my talk should draw to a close. I feel lucky that I can live 'outside' time restraints but realize that most people can't. I rarely have any idea of the time and never know what day it is!

On the other side when gatherings are to take place, someone will send a signal – a vibration – which is picked up by others who would attend. They pick up our timeline only by checking in, and the same signal is received from us when we think of our loved ones in heaven on our anniversaries, birthdays, weddings and get-togethers. We draw them close when we think of them.

Where is Heaven?

We like to think of heaven as 'up there', somewhere above us physically, but the truth is that the heavenly realms somewhat overlap our world here on earth. Heaven is literally all around us.

When leaving the body, the deceased feel they go through a tunnel of light which seems to whirl around them, but in fact what happens is that the space speeds up around them; like heaven, they too become a finer and finer substance and it's this speeded-up vibration which makes (for the most part) the heavenly realms invisible to the human eye.

Imagine how confusing it would be if we could see heaven overlap our earthly realms during our waking hours, right? When we are alive yet more in our spiritual bodies than our physical bodies (during sleep, when unconscious, when we are unwell or in a reverie, daydreaming or meditating, for example), the deceased can reach us more easily. This is why you are more likely to 'see', feel and sense the deceased during these times.

When the deceased appear in dream visitations and tell us that they are always with us, always around us, they mean it literally!

This next experience has several types of phenomenon so I have left them all in the story.

Offering Advice

Having just read your book *An Angel Held My Hand* cover to cover within a day I felt that I just had to email you with a few of my own experiences.

My very first experience was when I was fifteen years old. I had a dream that I was walking through a beautiful meadow with wild flowers and long grass. As I am walking along I come across a baby which is lying motionless in the grass and I come to realize that the baby has passed on. I continue to walk and I then come across a lady wearing a beautiful wedding dress. She stands there looking at me as if feeling a great deal of sadness. Still I continue to walk, unfazed. Next I come across my great-grandma lying in the grass wearing her blue nightdress. It suddenly dawns on me that she too has passed away.

My dream then shifts from the meadow to a hospital room and machines are bleeping loudly in the background as I stand looking at my great-grandma. I woke up after that moment. After going over my dream I came to realize that each person in the dream had a significant tie to my great-grandma. The baby was her daughter who died very young of meningitis, the lady in the wedding dress was her middle daughter who died of breast cancer aged only twenty-four. I only ever saw her wedding picture. Why my great-grandma was lying motionless in the grass I just couldn't work out. However, two weeks later I returned home from school to find my mother sitting in the dark and at that moment I knew my grandma had passed away. The dream then made complete sense to me. It was as if she was bringing me a warning.

The last words my great-grandma ever said to me as I was leaving her bedroom at the nursing home were 'Don't ever let your dad bother you, he isn't worth it.' I have always had a very strained relationship with my dad, it's true, and grandma knew this.

Three weeks after my great-grandma's passing I went to spend the day with my grandma (great-grandma's daughter), who has very strong psychic abilities. We sat at her dining table to have coffee and biscuits and she started talking to me about my dad. All of a sudden we heard an almighty bang. We searched around my grandma's bungalow for any evidence of something that might have caused such a loud bang and lastly we checked the bathroom. We discovered that my grandma's fabric pocket door tidy had fallen to the floor. What was most unusual was that the string to hold it up was intact and it had been hanging from a hook. It had to have been lifted for it to have fallen on the floor. [*JACKY: Sound familiar?*]

I still believe to this day that my great-grandma was giving us a sign to stop talking about my dad. Years went by with no experiences until two years ago when my half-brother was killed in a tragic accident. Since his passing I have experienced all kinds of things. I have been tapped on the shoulder, which at first I believed was my cat causing mischief. However, when I turned round to tell him off for pawing at me, instead of him sitting on the back of the sofa as I imagined I realized that he was actually sitting on the lawn in the garden!

Within five minutes I felt as though someone had blown directly in my ear and then my shoulder felt so cold I had goose flesh. By this point I started to believe my half-brother was still around so I decided to test him. I sat on the sofa with my laptop one afternoon, about to pay for my online lottery syndicate. I asked my dear half-brother to help me win some money that night. The next morning I checked the results and chuckled to myself when I found I had won seventy-five pence. The following week I asked the same thing. By now I was quite amused, so this time I asked him to please help me win some money but could it be something more substantial than 75 pence. The next morning I checked the results and found that I had won a huge £7.50. He died at twenty-three years of age and was quite a joker so I kindly thanked him and left it at that.

I also believe that I have met an angel. I was on my way to the most important interview I've ever had. I wanted a place on a course at university to study Health and Social Care. On my way to the interview I found that I was very early so I stopped and bought a coffee. I sat on a bench in a quiet part of the city centre. As I sat there going over in my head the possible questions I would be asked and how I would answer them, a man seemed to appear from nowhere (I didn't notice him approaching me anyway). He sat down next to me and asked me if I was on my way to an interview. I replied that I was and he asked what it was for. I told him my choice of course and he then proceeded to give me advice and interview tips. He told me that he used to be a doctor and was now a lecturer at the university and sometimes hosted interviews.

I found this information to be very useful indeed. The man was saying goodbye to me when suddenly I realized he was dressed oddly. He looked so out of place. He was wearing brown clothing and, even stranger, an Australian cork hat. At that moment my mobile phone started ringing so I quickly thanked the man and answered the call. It was my sister who lives in Australia (strangely enough). As I looked up, the man was nowhere to be seen. Needless to say, I got on to the course after following the advice of the 'Australian angel' sent to help me!

Coleen, Australia

The departed find so many ways and reasons to reach out to us. Maybe you've had an experience yourself and have only just remembered . . . or perhaps, like many others, after reading this book you'll have an experience! I hope you do. Heaven is so much closer than we can imagine.

And it's not only humans that come back to visit from heaven. Let's have a little look at some amazing stories of animals reaching out from the other side.

Animals and the Afterlife

'You think dogs will not be in heaven? I tell you,
they will be there long before any of us . . .'
Robert Louis Stevenson

For many of us, our animals are the creatures we love the most on earth! Even if you are lucky enough to have many wonderful human companions in life, the loss of a favourite pet can be as bad as the loss of a human loved one. Not everyone understands the loss but it's hard when a creature has been your constant companion for years and years, sitting by your side day in and day out. It's not surprising, therefore, that I receive many letters from people who worry about what happens to their pets after they pass on. Owners want to know the answers to the same questions they have about their lost human loved ones. 'Does my pet live on after death?' 'Will my pet be there to meet me once it's my time to leave the earth; will we be able to be together once more?' Incidentally, the quick answer is *yes* to all of the above!

My research shows me without a shadow of a doubt that pets continue after death in the same way that humans do. Pets have souls too . . . not exactly the same as humans (many of them have group souls – you only have to watch birds flock, bees swarm and fish shoal to know that they move almost as if with one mind). Other pets, like cats, dogs and horses, are more advanced souls and are already learning to see themselves as separate beings. Part of their role in living with us is for them to give us unconditional love while we treat them as individual souls and help them to separate from the collective souls they were once a part of.

Many animals, including some of my own, have visited their owners after they have physically passed away. Their grieving owners sense their pets around them, hear that familiar scratching, mewing or barking, or feel their pet rub up against their leg or jump upon their lap . . . they don't have to physically be around to do this!

The souls of pets interact just like human souls do; our animals can come back to visit from the other side to say goodbye and reassure us that they have a new life, that they haven't suddenly stopped existing. Best of all, some animals actually appear in the dream-visitation experiences that we've talked about earlier in the book. My dad often visited his daughters after his passing and brought family dogs with him. The souls of our passed-over loved ones can and do bring our recently lost pets with them too. Our pets want to connect with us in the same way that we connect with them. I've received hundreds of stories of pet visitation; they're magical encounters and extremely comforting to the bereaved.

I've heard stories of visits from dogs and cats (as you might expect), but also horses, rabbits, goats, parrots (and other birds), even a hamster! The pets communicate often by using some sort of symbolism or in a kind of telepathic way, that is, they don't move their mouths and talk like they might in a Disney film! (That would be funny, though, wouldn't it?) As humans receiving communication from our pets after death, we understand what they are trying to communicate with us and it often arrives as an idea-thought in our heads rather than actual words.

Our pets want us to know that they are safe on the other side and sometimes they want to simply say thank you to us for being their owner, especially if the pet was from a rescue centre. Your selflessness in rescuing them and giving them a good life is something to be grateful for. Your pet relishes the opportunity of saying thanks. Pets, like human loved ones, seem to be able to connect to our loss of them too. It seems strange, but if you have been up several times in the night crying, for example, or finding it difficult to concentrate at work, your pet will know this. They want to reassure us and let us know that they are safe. Pets sometimes appear to be visiting us alone but they are always brought forward by either spiritual guides or deceased loved ones. They are guided to us – they don't have the opportunity of getting lost during their earthly visit!

This story came from a Facebook follower. Sabrina was kind enough to share her experience with me (printed here with permission).

Happy and Healthy

I leased a horse a long time ago and he wasn't very nice; he bit and kicked out at everyone. One night

I was just drifting off to sleep and saw a picture of him in my mind. He looked really ill, and the next day when I got to the yard he'd been taken poorly.

After that day he changed; he let me near him and we finally became great friends. We were almost glued to each other's sides and he became so gentle . . . but only to me. Two years later he passed away. I was devastated and worried about what had become of him. That night I had a dream that he was healthy and running around a beautiful field; he looked so well and happy, but it was like I was watching through a frame and I couldn't touch him, just watch. I like to think it was him saying he remembered me.

Notice how Sabrina was unable to touch the horse. This story follows the human visitation experiences very closely.

Several other Facebook connections posted their experiences for me. Here they are:

Carmen – 'One of my cats, Rosie, visited me just before her son died . . . she put her paws on my leg just as she used to when she wanted attention. I spoke her name, said, "Hello, Rosie," and then she was gone!'

Tina – 'We lost our cat on New Year's Day, but Thursday night I dreamt that myself and Dad were walking around in town, and she was rubbing up against a corner wall of a shop. All we could say was, "She's come back to visit," and in the morning we found out Mum had dreamt of her the same night, too.'

Jennifer – 'One night whilst I half sat up in bed reading, I felt a cat walk up my legs. I put my hand out to stroke it and there was no cat there. My cat had been killed by my neighbour's two boys the year before. I know I didn't imagine it as it felt so real.'

Becky – 'We were lucky enough to live abroad and we used to look after dogs for other people. We were very fond of one particular dog called Rueben, who was a large chocolate Labrador. He sadly passed over, but he comes and visits us; we can smell him in our car, yes, that lovely wet dog smell! And at times we feel his wet nose on our feet.'

Christine – 'We had a beautiful Labrador mix for over fifteen years. Her name was Missy. Towards the end of her life, she couldn't walk any more, and stopped eating. We had her put down in July 2009. Missy used to be very well known because we could always hear her coming by the *tick, tick, tick* of her nails on the hard wood floors. For months after she was gone we were always hearing her nails on the floor. My husband and I would look at each other and just smile because we knew she was here with us.'

Nadia-Salvatore – 'My cat visited me in a dream. I was going about my normal day and she knocked on the door! When I opened it she was being held by an angel and put her paws out for a hug like a human would. I sobbed so much as I held her and woke up crying because I missed her so much. I know she's watching over me.'

Claire – 'I lost my beloved cat Charlie just over three years ago and dreamt about him loads. One night I dreamt that he was walking down our road towards our gates; I opened the gates and picked him up and he was really healthy and fat, as he was before he became ill. I had a cuddle with him and told him how well he looked. I haven't dreamt about him since and I'm sure he came back to tell me he was OK.'

Melda – 'When our dog Paddy passed away we were in so much grief, but we both had the same dream that two versions of Paddy were sitting on the bed: one full of life and the other not. I think it was his way of letting us know he was OK and back to himself. When he passed away the vets sent us a sympathy card, but after the dream we got another one exactly the same. It seemed a strange coincidence. We used to hear him jumping on and off the bed. Even visitors heard it.

One day my little niece came to visit. She'd never seen Paddy whilst he was alive. She was only two and she kept pointing to the back door and saying,

"Paddy, Paddy," as if he were outside. She was crying so I picked her up and went to the back door with her. I asked her, "Where is Paddy?" and she pointed to where she could see him. As I went to tell the others she put her finger up to her lips and started shaking her head as if it were a secret. She didn't want me to tell the others what she had seen. I am convinced that it really was Paddy coming to visit us again.'

Some people find they dream that they have visited their pet on the other side. Mainly it's the kind of 'halfway' stopover full of bright-coloured grass and green, green trees with beautiful flowers and sparkling water . . . all of which seems to be alive and full of that kind of vitality that makes people say that heaven is more real than the place where we live now, as if heaven is our real home and earth is somewhere we just stay for a while. Heaven is just as beautiful for pets as it is for humans!

Signs From Animals

Now we've seen a few real-life contact experiences from our pets on heaven-side, let's have a look at how pets tend to let us know that they are around. Here are a few things to look out for, or things you may already have experienced:

- You'll wake from a sleep to feel your pet jump upon your bed (if this is something they would have done in life). Cats will walk around in a circle to 'bed in' and you might feel the weight of your dog on your legs. Sometimes when people switch on the light they may even notice a distinct outline of where they felt the pet was lying, even though they were unable to actually see their pet once they awoke. When watching television or reading (or other distracting activities), the owner will feel their pet rub up against their leg or other body part and unconsciously reach out to stroke the pet before remembering that the animal has passed away. The sensation of fur, skin, scales or feathers is so real that the owner forgets that their pet has passed away. Has this happened to you?

- The owner might hear a sound which they automatically associate with the pet: nails scratching on a hard-wood floor, or tapping or scratching at a door or window, asking to be let in. Other sounds might include the cat flap opening and closing (occasionally attributed to the wind), a familiar bark, growl or snuffle, or the sound of a pet bell (hanging from a spirit collar).
- The pet might be seen out of the corner of your eye, running outside in the garden or snuggled up in its favourite corner or chair. I remember walking into my mum and dad's old bungalow twelve months after their faithful dog Suzi had passed. I distinctly saw her run towards me in greeting and felt her waggy tail flick against my

leg. In discussion with family members I discovered that others had experienced the same sensation. The phenomenon would occur several times over a three-to-four-year period.

- Some owners still smell their pets after they pass away. That familiar wet dog scent might not necessarily be a good one though!

- My dog Lady appeared to me in a dream several weeks after she had passed away. I found myself in a heavenly space with my little dog appearing to show me how happy she was now she had been released from her old body. Sadly, I'd had to make the difficult decision to have her euthanized and carried a lot of guilt as we all do. Lady was showing grateful thanks that I made my decision out of love. She showed me that she was now like a puppy again (she actually looked younger than I had ever seen her as we adopted her as a rescue dog when she was several years old). She bounced around and in the distance were many other family dogs we'd loved and lost. It was a wonderfully comforting experience. Maybe you've had something like this happen to you?

- You might pick up a sign in another form. For example, you may think of your pet over several days and then when you are out and about you hear an owner call his pet by the same name as your dog. Maybe you see a photograph on the front of a book or in a magazine and it reminds you very strongly of your animal. Sometimes it's just the look in their eyes. Maybe you'll find a white feather appear in an unusual place after you've asked for your pet to appear. There are so many more ways that this might happen, so be alert! Remember the Pluto dog story earlier in the book? Your pet may come up with their own special signs – with a little help from their animal angels in heaven, of course.

When pets visit us from heaven they often appear as their younger selves . . . just like humans do. I was thrilled to see Lady as a puppy. I recall even now how fluffy she looked! It was as if she'd got wet and been blown dry with a hairdryer! Their aim is to show us that they are in good (perfect) health now and that they are happy and well. If your pet had been ill you can expect that he or she might appear to bounce around or chase after a ball, for example – anything to indicate their fit and healthy existence now.

How to Experience Afterlife Contact From Your Pet

It's possible to encourage a dream-visitation experience by simply asking for one, but it's useful to make a connection with your pet first of all. The emotion of love acts as a carrier for your need for contact. Here are a few ideas on how you might do this.

1. If you are lucky enough to have a photograph of your pet, you can hold this and use it to recall the feelings of love you shared with them and how much he or she meant to you. If not, you can still do this experience: build up either the image of your pet or the feelings you shared . . . closing your eyes really helps with this. Imagine that the thread of love that connected you is still secure; work your way along the thread until you reach your pet. Feel the love that connects you and let it envelope you like a giant hug. Relax and enjoy this loving contact.

2. If this type of visualization is challenging for you, creating a scrapbook of memories might work better. Gather up photos, pictures of similar animals or pictures from the Internet or magazines that represent the essence of your pet (fluffy, comical ears or maybe images of the same breed), and stick them down along with poems and memories of your time together. You could create specific pages:

   - Food that my pet liked to eat: cut out pictures from magazines, list or draw pictures – even photograph a pet-food label on your next trip to the supermarket!
   - Photographs: Here is the type of bedding and collars/leads/saddle I would have bought for my pet if money had been no object (include pictures or descriptions).

- Pictures of the type of toys your pet would have liked/bowl your fish might have swum in, etc.
- Little paragraphs about the things your pet did that made you laugh or smile.
- Stories of fun days that you and your pet had when, for example, you would sit together snuggled up in front of the fire.

You get the idea. You can buy a scrap book or make your own by stapling together several strong sheets of coloured paper. Make a pretty cover and write your pet's name on the front.

3. Build a website in your pet's honour.
4. Raise some money for a pet charity in your pet's name (coffee morning, fundraising run, sponsored swim, or something pet-related – a sponsored dog walk maybe?).
5. Sit quietly. Before you go to sleep is the ideal time. Imagine your pet is standing in front of you (swimming, flying, as appropriate). In your head, tell your pet how much they meant to you and how much you miss them. As you do this you may find you get a little emotional – that's OK, it's part of the process. Ask that they try to find a way of reaching out to you to let you know that they are safe and well in their new home.

You might experience one of the following:

- A great sense of peace surrounds you – this is your pet reaching out to you!

- A strong connection there and then. You know as that tear runs down your face that your pet's soul is close by.
- A visit comes in the form of a dream visitation (a real visit from the soul whilst your body is physically asleep). It might take several days or weeks for conditions to be right for this to happen.
- You pick up a sign from your pet some time over the next few days (a feather, or you hear someone say their name, etc. – as above).
- You hear, sense or see your pet, or a young child or other family pet becomes aware of their presence.

Bugs and Things

This next experience is very unusual but, as with all these stories, the unusual tales are very familiar to me. I've heard them all before! Is it a sign? It might well be!

Goodbye . . . and Hello Again

On New Year's Day we had our beloved dog Molly put to sleep. She had developed skin cancer and it was spreading rapidly. Her breathing was becoming laboured, a sure sign that the cancer was spreading to her lungs. Rather than let Molly suffer and be in pain, we made a heartbreaking yet conscious decision to let her go to sleep for the last time on the earth plane. She drifted off peacefully.

Molly had lived with my eldest daughter because technically, although everyone loved her, she was my daughter's dog. As you can imagine, after having Molly for almost twelve years, my daughter was devastated. However, a strange thing happened to her and her fiancé yesterday. A fly, of all things, suddenly appeared out of nowhere and it was unusually brave. My daughter's fiancé went towards it and it flew away, but when my daughter approached it, the fly actually allowed her to touch it and it didn't move! Now that never happens in real life, does it!?

I do believe in the afterlife but have never been fortunate enough to experience anything personally (well, nothing that I can be sure of). My daughter's fiancé made a passing comment that the fly could be Molly and even though my daughter doesn't believe, she was somewhat taken aback by the unusual actions of the fly. The fly just seemed to sit there watching her.

When they told me, I smiled to myself because I do believe this was Molly's way of letting my daughter know that she had arrived safely on the other side . . . I would love your thoughts on this – do you think this could be a sign from Molly?

Michaela, England

I do! You know, Michaela, this is where people will say, 'Seriously, Jacky? Are you crazy?' but yes, I do think it's possible. If people experience butterflies and dragonflies as signs from the afterlife, then why not flies too ... if appropriate? Years ago, one reader had a fly land on the book she was reading; it walked along a specific set of words in a pattern on the page, spelling out the comforting message she had longed to hear from the afterlife! It's not for me to judge either way; what is wonderful is that the family gained comfort from the experience.

Here is another experience that a family found comforting. This one comes from Canada.

The Friendly Butterfly

We were staying at our cottage for the weekend; my husband, daughter and my son-in-law were sitting on the balcony, and all of the sudden, a butterfly (a Grand Monarch) started flying around us. I have to admit that this was not the first time that a Grand Monarch has flown around me but this time felt different, special; I even wondered for the first time if I might be able to touch one.

The butterfly decided to rest on the balcony ramp, so I put my finger next to him and, to my great surprise, he climbed on to my finger. I touched his wing very gently and he seemed to like it. As my daughter was next to me I suggested she put her finger next to mine and the butterfly immediately climbed on to her finger, and she was able to gently touch the wing as well. Then we watched as it flew away.

My husband and son-in-law were so surprised to watch what had happened that they said if they hadn't seen it with their own eyes they would not have believed us. After reading the stories of butterflies in your book we found our experience very reassuring.

Sylvie, Canada

Imagine you yourself had passed away and wanted to pop back from heaven to reassure your loved ones that you were OK and had made it safely to the other side of life. Of course there are rules: you can't frighten your loved ones back on earth and you mustn't make things worse for them so that they grieve more for you after the experience. Wouldn't a simple encounter like one of these comfort them more than, say, fully manifesting in front of them, potentially causing a heart attack?!

When you look at these contacts logically it really makes sense that they are so subtle. Often over time people have more and more, and stronger and stronger visits from loved ones and pets in the afterlife. As we get used to the phenomenon, our deceased loved ones can try less subtle experiences. Just reading this book will help. Your new awareness of these things will help you to be less afraid, knowing that contact from the other side is simply a loving gift. The afterlife is real and you are entitled to be comforted by its existence just like everyone else. If this has not happened to you yet, then even the reading of this book will take you one step closer to your goal.

Butterflies are such a common sign that I wanted to include a couple more for you. Here is the next one.

Butterfly Bombers

In December last year my mum lost a sister to cancer, followed by a second sister passing in February, again with cancer. On 6 June my mum was diagnosed with cancer too. Since Mum's diagnosis we've had two plain white butterflies flying in and around the garden. We often said they were Mum's sisters coming to visit and it eased our sadness.

Sadly, we lost Mum on 12 August. On the day of Mum's passing nobody noticed the butterflies around, but on the following day we noticed they had come back and were joined by a third. The newest addition was white with dark edging on its wings. We see the three of them flying together and sometimes the newest one comes along on its own.

When we registered Mum's passing at the register office we were obviously upset. But as we left the building we were almost dive-bombed by a very similar-looking butterfly that kept flying around us. We like to think that the butterflies are a sign and we've enjoyed them coming to visit us.

Darren, England

Wonderful, right? OK, here is another great butterfly story. I'm not sure that this one is so subtle though! What do you think?

Butterflies and Birds

I suffer with ME and recently spent a spell in bed. I was reading your book *An Angel By My Side* and you mentioned that flickering lights is one of the afterlife signs. I was particularly tearful and fed up because I was feeling ill. Anyway, I started to read the story and, as I did so, my bedside lamp started to flicker; when I looked up there was a Red Admiral butterfly! I was amazed at the coincidence but I did feel comforted by it.

Two days later I was in bed asleep and I was woken up by a sound behind the curtain. When I looked I couldn't believe it, it was another Red Admiral butterfly! That evening my husband had a shower and, as he put on his dressing gown, guess what happened? A Red Admiral flew out of the sleeve! I truly believe that someone was letting me know they were there and it helped greatly.

Karen, who sent me the above story, shared another experience with me and, as it is animal-related, I decided to include it here too.

Bird Sign

In 1982 my dear brother Keith died in a motorcycle accident. He lived with my parents and on the evening he died I phoned their house and he answered. All I said was, 'Hi, can I speak to Mum please?' I didn't ask him how his day was or anything and I have always beaten myself up about it.

My husband and I celebrated our twenty-fifth wedding anniversary in 2006 and took Sam, our daughter, and her boyfriend Tom, and our sons Simon and James to Mauritius with us to renew our vows. Sam had given me a lovely book to take with me and it was full of heart-warming stories. I started to read it, relaxing by the pool with the family, and I read a story about a mum's son who had gone to work that morning on his motorbike and sadly died. The mother never forgave herself for not telling her son she loved him that morning. It was too much and reminded me of that fateful day with Keith. I burst into tears and the family came over to see if I was OK.

Bryan, my husband, was comforting me as I told them about the story in the book. I said that I would love to have a sign like the one in the book to show me that Keith knew I loved him. At that exact moment a dove flew over and landed between our feet! If that's not proof then I don't know what is. Not just one feather but a whole dove-full!

Karen, England

Isn't that a fun story? I love Karen's quote too, 'not just one feather but a whole dove-full'. I may have to use that quote again! Here is another really gentle sign which brought this reader massive comfort.

Feather Sign

I had just finished reading one of your books but I didn't really have any faith in the existence of the other side because I'd never had an experience myself. Then, sadly, my lovely cat Crunchie passed away; it sounds stupid but I found it hard to bring myself to accept that he had passed. I'd read in your book that white feathers are a sign of the other side coming back to see you. Then one day not long afterwards I was cleaning the kitchen and noticed there was a white feather on the cooker; now the cooker was Crunchie's favourite place to sit. I know he felt like a king being so high up and overlooking the dogs. Do you know what? Once I found the feather I knew he was OK. It was exactly the sign I had been looking for!

Chelsea, England

Would any old feather found in any place have been as comforting? Probably not. It shows that the time and place of these little signs can be really important. These simple experiences mean little to other people but they're not meant to. I want you to see that you don't need to tell anyone else about what happens to you if you don't want to. Your own connection to the heavenly side is personal and private; there is certainly no need to convince anyone else of the truth of your experience!

When we ask for the sign and then the sign appears, that is the proof we need. Even subtle signs from the creatures above can have great meaning if the timing is right. I could go on and on with this section and people are so interested in the animal stories that I have included animal sections in most of my books. All good things must come to an end, although I couldn't finish this chapter without sharing one last experience.

So, finally, here is a story sent to me by Trudie.

Hugs

Beauty was a tiny crossbreed puppy that fitted into the palm of our twelve-year-old daughter's hand. Right from the start Beauty was convinced that she was a much bigger dog. Every day she would sit on the back doorstep guarding the house just like a bigger dog would have done. Beauty was extremely affectionate, loyal and caring, and always liked to know where we were in the house and would come to look for us if she hadn't seen us in a while.

When I had my first breast cancer operation in 2006 she stayed by my side for the two weeks I was off work and wouldn't let me out of her sight; it was as if on some level she knew that I was unwell. She was there by my side again when I had another operation for a recurrence in 2008, and as a result of chronic pain complications I've actually been off work since – although I was never left alone for long.

Beauty was my constant companion despite getting older; in her later years she developed arthritis and became a bit deaf. She also developed a heart murmur and last November she was diagnosed with diabetes too. Beauty always seemed to bounce back quickly and never 'complained' about her daily injections. Sadly, in May of this year she developed pancreatitis and eventually we had to make the painful decision to have her put to sleep at the age of fifteen. It was a really difficult thing to do but we knew we were doing the best for our faithful friend.

I stayed by her side holding her until her last breaths and knelt in front of her so that I was the last thing she saw as she closed her eyes.

We miss her so much but I sometimes think I hear her around the house, probably looking for us still. My husband had a very vivid dream a few weeks ago where he was hugging Beauty and holding her; she was licking his face and 'kissing' him. He said it felt more real than any dream he's ever had! I'm sure this was a visitation.

Trudie, England

I'm sure too. It's that 'more real than real' comment that seems to give these dream visitations (real spirit visits) away. Spirit contacts, whilst the body is asleep, are always retained in the memory long after normal dreams fade away, so that they can be treasured forever. Even so, I do like to keep a record of my own experiences (and regular readers will see them sprinkled throughout my books!). Don't forget to record your experiences too . . . you know it can even encourage more to occur!

Perhaps thankfully we are unable to go to heaven to

visit our loved ones as a matter of everyday occurrence (and I include pets in this category). I guess for the most part it would be a dangerous thing to do. We have to live out our lives on this side of the divide, but it's wonderful when we can be comforted by these little signs from heaven. When our beloved pets can no longer be with us here on this side of life, isn't it amazing the way they are able to bring us comfort from the afterlife? As with our human friends, that loving connection never ends. Love continues on the other side.

Over and over again people write and tell me how their grief was eased after such experiences. If that is the case, then their work is well and truly done. Thank you, beloved pets!

OK, now I'd really like to explore some of the more bizarre phenomena. I think you're ready! Remember to keep an open mind. I appreciate that the things I am sharing in this book may seem 'too good to be true' but might I reassure you that every single story *is* true and that all of my 'ideas' and 'assumptions' are based on personal experience and years of research. There is so much we don't truly understand about the world around us – it might seem hard to fathom but it doesn't mean it isn't true! Are you ready to stretch your mind a little more? Then read on . . .

Life, But Not as We Know it

'The miracles on earth are the laws of heaven.'

Jean Paul

Do we always die when it's 'our time' or can mistakes happen? Yes! Sadly 'mistakes' do happen. We might take our own life, for example, fail to heed warnings when a serious illness strikes or not be paying attention when walking near a busy road or cliff edge. Not everything is set in stone; we are born with great potential but we still have to live out that potential, make choices and choose the transportation!

Here is another story.

Mistakes Can Happen

I was watching your and Madeline's Q&A video on *Call Me When You Get to Heaven* and I was reminded of a dream I used to have quite often. [*JACKY: This is a promotional video on YouTube for the book I wrote with my sister.*]

I would dream that I was with my sister, Yvonne, who passed when she was twenty-two and I was twenty. The dreams varied but we were always doing ordinary things together, usually having fun. Towards the end of these dreams I would suddenly turn to her and say something like, 'Hang on . . . you died . . .' and she would say, 'Yes, it was a mistake, that's why I was allowed to come back.'

As the years went on with the dreams taking the same turn towards the end, she almost used to get impatient, saying, 'How many times do I have to explain?' Over the past few years I haven't had these dreams so often but when I do have them there's one thing that never changes – I never remember that she has died until the dream is nearly at an end.

Jennie, England

These experiences, as we've already discovered, can seem more real than real life. Yvonne has been given permission to visit her sister from the other side and as in life they are able to share real-life family occasions. It seems likely that Yvonne would have influenced Jennie in various ways had she lived. By visiting in dreams she is able to do this still, although in a more subconscious way. The fact that Jennie *does* remember Yvonne is 'dead' eventually is what makes us so sure that this is a dream visitation and not a normal dream!

Reality is Not What it Seems

I really wanted to have a look at this next idea to help you open your mind even more. I want you to be able to think hard about life . . . which is not always what it seems.

As humans, we feel most comfortable when the world around us conforms to a set of rules. Rules make us feel safe in an otherwise confusing life. We (most of us) like a certain amount of timetabled activity: our favourite programme on at the same time each week; knowing what time to pick the kids up from school every day or always eating the same meal on a Sunday. We prefer this way of life to the point that, as we get older, it's easier to become 'set in our ways'. Thank goodness for children, grandchildren and pets to shake things up a bit. Nothing is always going to be as you planned with a pet or child in your life!

OK, so children and animals cause small, unexpected changes (they want to eat when you didn't plan to, they make a mess you have to clean up and so on, but these are small things really). Real life doesn't always conform to the greater rules, however. Worst of all, your reality is challenged when 'you know' for sure that something is a certain way, then all of a sudden you discover it isn't at all! Sometimes it's like we've stepped into some sort of twilight zone or alternative reality.

I loved doing research for this section. What do you think of these experiences?

Parallel Universe?

You may have heard of the theory of parallel universes. The theory goes that at each juncture in our life we make a life choice or choose a path, and our life flows along in that direction. However, what if we made a different choice? With parallel universes it's said that one part of us continues on with the alternative choice (getting married rather than concentrating on our career; or having children rather than remaining childless, for example). If this theory is to be believed we could easily end up with millions, billions of different lives going on all at the same time. Of course we have no idea if this is true or not . . . or do we?

A Spanish woman woke up one morning to notice subtle differences in her life. As far as Lerina was aware, she hadn't been ill or been in an accident but her whole life was subtly different to the one that existed before she went to bed the night before. The first thing she noticed was that her bed sheets were different. She thought it was strange but didn't over-analyse the situation until she went to work.

She went to her usual office and discovered that her normal desk was no longer in its place, her name no longer listed on the door. Confused, she looked herself up on the internal computer network and discovered she still worked at the same company that she'd worked at for twenty years but in a different department than the one she recalled and with a different boss, one she didn't know.

Lerina went to her doctor and was given numerous tests, all of which found nothing wrong, yet her partner of seven years whom she'd split up with several months earlier was now back in her life and her new partner no longer existed. Even a private detective could find no trace of her recent love or his family.

Does that story give you chills? It did me! Imagine if

this had happened to you? I found it both fascinating and terrifying at the same time. OK, now let's have a tiny look at another strange phenomenon.

Different Lives

Do you believe in reincarnation? Can you imagine the possibility that we as souls move from one life to the next, one after the other? I do – now – and I know my friend Jenny does too. What do you think of her story? A close friend of mine, author and columnist Jenny Smedley, is a totally normal and rational woman yet she recalls and shared with me a totally bizarre experience that seems beyond explanation. Here is her story in her own words (used with permission).

Which Life Am I In?

Have you ever woken up and wondered for a second which house you were in? This has happened to me a few times as we've moved house quite a lot. But one morning I couldn't remember which LIFE I was in. For about thirty seconds I was totally unnerved by not knowing who I was. Then I saw [my husband] Tony lying next to me and I recognized this soul instantly. With that, just like an old-fashioned librarian skimming through a sheaf of book cards, I found my mind skimming through a sheaf of past lives. They flicked through, very fast, and then suddenly I came to the right one. *Oh*, I thought, *I'm JENNY!* Not ME, but

Jenny, as if Jenny was but one part of me. It was quite scary until I realized what had happened!

Past Lives

I don't want to devote a big section to this phenomenon here because there are loads of brilliant books on the subject if you want to do your own research. It seemed important to mention it though, so here is a little background.

Many people, children in particular, have memories of past lives. I myself recall several. One came to me as a sort of very real dream, another whilst I was under hypnosis, and other snippets of lives I have recalled spontaneously. I am certainly not alone in this.

I love the research that some scientists and researchers have done regarding past lives and past-life recall, particularly with children. A youngster, usually under school age, will suddenly blurt out a memory that seems to have no bearing on their current life. For example, 'Mummy, do you remember when I was your mother and you were my child . . . when we were here before?' Or, 'Do you see that house over there, Dad? I used to live there with my wife years ago and it had a yellow door . . .' It gives you goose bumps, doesn't it? Most of these memories spontaneously recalled by youngsters are forgotten by school age (although some retain the memories their whole life long).

If youngsters in your own life share these types of experiences it is well worth jotting them down. A casual, vague interest from you (as if you are also concentrating on something else), with gentle questioning, might bring up more details – although it might also shut down the subject altogether! What is interesting though is that occasionally the child has no memory of the conversation afterwards, as if they drop momentarily into an altered state of consciousness (like daydreaming), which has opened some sort of doorway into this hidden knowledge of the higher mind.

Past-life recall just shows the journey of the soul. We are born, die and return to heaven-side. Then, when it's 'time', we are born again in a different body with the same groups of souls playing out different lives or parts . . . like a play. That's a very simplistic way of putting it, of course. The truth is way more complicated than that – but perhaps I'll write another book on the subject one day!

Some investigators have followed up and even 'interviewed' toddlers about their past-life memories. By following up the clues they have indeed found living relatives from previous lives who have verified even the most minute of details given by the child who, in this life at least, has never met the people concerned. In some cases the youngster has never been to the country in question – not in this life, anyway! At least one researcher believes they have proved that reincarnation is a reality, and I certainly believe it's true.

In one of my own past lives (the one that came to me when I was under hypnosis), several of my relatives, including one of my sisters, shared the life with me. Many years later, not knowing about my past-life hypnosis memory, my sister, quite independently, had a dream in which she appeared to recall the exact same life. It was only when she shared her 'strange dream' with me that I went and got my notes from my regression many years earlier. We were astonished when we compared notes and realized that we'd both glimpsed a life where we had been servants in a big house . . . the same house! (I have written about this and all of my paranormal experiences in several of my other books).

Before we move on I want to include one more story here. This is a past-life experience which Donna shared with me.

Lives Remembered

I know I've two past lives at least; in one of them I died in a concentration camp (Auschwitz) in World War Two. I remembered this life when I was about six years old. Years went past then one day at school, in a history lesson, I told my teacher everything about the gas chamber where I'd died. The colour in his face drained. He pulled me to one side, asking me how I knew about this place. When I told him I'd died there, he was amazed as he'd visited the place and knew all the details that I was confirming to him.

Donna, England

Donna's story is another one that makes you shiver! When your brain can't find another solution to the story, it doesn't mean it isn't true, remember. I can't explain everything here but do continue to keep an open mind.

Time Slips

Other people have experienced what can only be described as a 'time slip'. Reality as we know it seems to disappear for a few seconds (or minutes), only to be replaced by visions of another time. Here are a couple of random examples I discovered during research.

As I walked past the church I became immediately aware of what felt like a bubble ripple around the high street, at very high speed, and the high street changed . . . the people that were walking in the high street vanished and were replaced with a smaller selection of people dressed in Victorian attire. The whole event lasted no more than ten to fifteen seconds before everything returned to what I can only call normal . . .

This next experience coincidentally occurred to someone who lived less than ten miles from where I was living at the time of the incident.

A painter and decorator living in Staffordshire, England, was driving along in his car when he began to feel unwell. He felt light-headed and his 'left ear hurt and felt hot'. Pulling over to the side of the road, he noticed that night had suddenly become day and the road in front of him had disappeared. In front of him now instead of road he saw only fields and trees. Soldiers in civil war clothing were fighting each other right in front of him but his vehicle seemed invisible to them. He was terrified but luckily, a few seconds later, he found himself back at the side of the road – everything had returned to normal.

Now that was really spooky, but the world is created in a way we don't fully understand . . . though we're working on it! Life is not seamless and perfect, even if we want it to be. Sometimes people stray across the cracks!

Nikola Tesla

Truth sometimes, it is said, can be stranger than fiction and this is certainly the case with the strange works of the late inventor Nikola Tesla. His research may explain some of the above phenomena. During his lifetime he worked alongside both Thomas Edison and Guglielmo Marconi. He worked on inventions including motors, radios, X-ray tubes, fluorescent lighting, robotics, radar, aircraft, missiles and energy weapons. His biggest dream was the wireless transmission of electricity. Even today, some of the things he worked on are not fully understood – not by you and I at least – but they exist nevertheless!

He was as brilliant as he was strange. Working in Colorado Springs, Tesla realized the earth itself was 'a conductor of limitless dimensions' and he created constructions to harness and manipulate this. Outside the building where he experimented with this energy he was able to power bulbs without the use of wires whilst inside the building ball lightning would appear; horses walking nearby were said to have picked up electric shocks through their hooves.

In 1895, Tesla was said to have made the discovery that time and space could be influenced by using charged, rotating magnetic fields; this all came about as a result of his work with radio frequencies and the transmission of electrical energy through the atmosphere. Tesla also conducted secret time-zone experiments, discovering that time and space could be warped, creating doorways that could lead to other time zones.

Tesla claimed he'd received radio signals from outside of the planet, bravely suggesting Mars or Venus. These claims didn't help his reputation one bit, but this isn't all. Tesla's research was apparently used in a series of experiments carried out on behalf of the US Navy. The so-called 'Philadelphia Experiment' is one which many sources deny, yet it seems to have stood the test of time, with many books having been written about the subject . . . I've even mentioned it in a previous book of mine.

The experiment was based on Einstein's unified field theory. The story goes that the Navy wanted to use this theory to 'bend light' around objects (warships, for example) to make them appear invisible. The so-called 'Philadelphia Experiment' (15 August 1943), with the destroyer escort USS *Eldridge*, was a disaster and did much more than make the ship 'seem' to disappear. During the experiment, a green fog appeared around the ship before the ship itself disappeared from Philadelphia only to briefly appear in Norfolk Harbor (where it had originally started), some saying it had briefly gone back in time. Reports suggest that many of the crew became embedded in the walls of the ship, as if they had dematerialized and then rematerialized, blending somehow with the fabric of the ship. Others were said to have gone insane as a result of the experience, with many more of the crew said to have been shot, with no one knowing what to do with them. Some of them simply vanished.

Is the story true? I can't say, but I can tell you that after Tesla's death his notes were confiscated by the FBI! Sadly, Tesla died almost penniless on 7 January 1943. No doubt his research has continued behind closed doors since then. Our world is certainly not what it seems.

Floating Fogs

Certain places around the earth attract more than their fair share of paranormal phenomena too. The Devil's Triangle (sometimes known as the Dragon's Triangle) is an area of the globe located near Miyake Island, south of Tokyo, reaching over to Guam. It's the exact opposite side of the world to the area known as the Bermuda Triangle; both are sections of ocean where ships, people and planes disappear, often accompanied by a mysterious fog (maybe this is the same fog created by Tesla or something similar?).

Green or blue fog seems to be at the heart of other strange phenomena around the world, especially with regard to the time slips mentioned above. Are these floating fogs appearing as a result of experiments in this same phenomenon and are they altering the time and space around them? Researcher Jenny Randles wrote about a fascinating story in her book *Time Storms*. What happened to the lady in the following account? Military experiment, alien abduction or something else? Read on.

Dawn, the young wife of a colonel in the Royal Engineers, was travelling to India with her husband and a group of Gurkhas to visit with the Dalai Lama. It was 1947 and the hazardous journey involved travelling over desert plains and mountain ranges.

One day the young woman was sitting in the truck when the air around her became icy cold. Others had noticed it too and she recalls feeling as if someone were touching her. A cloud-like shape appeared in the sky before floating towards them; the Gurkhas seemed frozen with shock but her husband rushed towards the object with a gun; he fell to the floor as if he had run into an invisible wall. It was at this point that the woman felt her muscles go rigid and the strange cloud seemed to float around them. She described it as being as big as a house. Time, she says, seemed to lose importance, though the experience felt as if it lasted some while; her hair stood on end as there seemed to be an electrical tingle around her. As she came out of the experience, nightfall was almost upon them. Time had been lost during the experience, and many were left feeling sick afterwards; some of the team came out in a rash which lasted until the following day.

Sadly, following their frightening experience, the party decided to turn back and never completed their trip to visit the Dalai Lama. This indicates that the experience had created much fear in the party. Luckily (as far as we are aware), no one suffered any long-term effects from the encounter.

Lives Between Lives

Here is another strange phenomenon which seems to bring consistent results over and over again. Under hypnosis, many thousands of people have recalled a time when they were in the heavenly realms; a life between lives. Their stories are remarkably similar to each other.

One woman wrote to tell me that her young daughter spontaneously recalls picking her life and choosing her parents before she was ultimately born into the life she is living now. She chose to incarnate into her current life to help her father. In the heavenly realms she was shown a young boy who stood helpless as his young sister was burnt to death. The experience scarred the young boy and he forever had difficulties interacting with and befriending other youngsters. Now this boy was a man and she picked this life knowing that as the daughter of this man he might have challenges accepting her into his life. She chose to incarnate anyway.

Many years on, he is a wonderful father and now grandfather, her presence eventually helping to heal the trauma he suffered as a young boy. Isn't it wonderful to know that we choose our lives not just for the personal growth of our own souls but to assist others on their own path? When you are struggling with your own life, stop and think: did I partly pick this life to help someone else? It will surely ease your burden somewhat. I like to ask myself that question whenever something seems to go wrong, 'Why did I choose to experience this in my life?' Usually there is a great lesson to be learnt somewhere!

Years ago I had an email from a lady who recalls her life before being born. Because I have given so many other details here I have left out her full name and year of birth for privacy (as she requested).

Picking My Life Before Being Born

I remember quite a bit about the time when I was preparing to be born into this lifetime. I remember waiting and waiting and asking and asking about the things that I was meant to be doing, as well as wanting information about the people who were going to be born into the same life as me.

I remember that I was supposed to wait to be born with this group; they were the people from my group, the ones that I had been training with. I know this sounds strange but we went through lessons in heaven, all types of lessons, but they were all for spiritual advancement. Although I wanted to wait for my group, I also missed the earth existence: tasting, smelling things, touching someone physically and so on.

We were able to view certain aspects of the life to come in advance. I remember being warned before going into the building with the 'viewer' that I was advancing well and if I went to a human life without my group-mates I might be 'set back' quite a bit. They told me that I would probably be lonely because the people I really 'connect' with wouldn't be there for another ten to fifteen years.

Yet there was still something that pulled me to a human existence much stronger than wanting to stay and wait for my group. My very best friend on the other side, the one that I did everything with, decided to stay and wait but I decided to go ahead.

I chose a date and time of birth, 31 October, and the year. They showed me choices that I had. I remember being told that I had eight lives to choose from because I had already experienced the other events and lessons that would be learnt by the other humans that were being born on that day. I was able to view the lives that had been set. I remember there were a few that I was horrified at, but I was told to remember my training and to remember that I could change the outcomes by making different choices, and that the lives wouldn't turn out the way that they were shown to me on the viewer.

I decided to pick a mid-range life where things would be fairly simple yet I would face some challenges. I tell you, my mind keeps going to a life that I was shown as a black man shot down in the middle of a street at the age of sixteen. I don't know why that choice sticks out though, because I didn't choose that life. [*JACKY: I wonder if this short life had been offered because it would still give this lady the opportunity of reincar-*

nating again with her soul-group members she had left behind; meaning they could still all be together?]

I remember being shown the parent choices that I had, and the growing-up conditions. I chose my parents and a middle-class life. I remember that all of my choices happened in a matter of hours and once everything was decided I can't remember leaving the room or what happened next. After that I recall complete darkness, a long 'chute' that I fell through, and then the time I was born, exactly as I remembered it beforehand.*

'T', USA

I hope you didn't find this chapter too disturbing. The existence of a heavenly realm is surely just the 'tip of the iceberg' when it comes to discovering our life behind life. Who are we? Where did we come from and why are we here? So many future books!

OK, we've explored all sorts of things so far, including the afterlife adventures of my readers and my conclusions relating to them. What about other cultures around the world? Each has its own traditional view of what heaven might be like. I couldn't really begin to cover them all but I thought we might take a little peck at some of them. Will it affect your own views on what you believe? Maybe your religion already tells you what heaven is like? Let's see . . .

---

* If you are interested in more information about choosing your life before life (or 'interlife' information), my favourite book on the subject is *Life Between Lives* by Dr Michael Newton.

A Worldwide View of Heaven

'Go to Heaven for the climate,
Hell for the company.'

Mark Twain

Each country, each culture and every religion has their own unique view of what the afterlife may be like. It seems likely that these experiences are based at least in part on spiritual encounters or near-death experiences had by somebody at some point in the culture at some time or other; as well as information passed down through religious and spiritual leaders.

Some afterlife 'knowledge' shared will no doubt have been as a result of keeping the peace or maintaining order amongst the masses. If your god was one that harmed wrongdoers, wouldn't it help to keep control of the wayward public? Who'd want to go to another world when they died if they were likely to be punished? If you had to keep order amongst large numbers of people, I imagine the threat of punishment after inevitable death would have been very useful indeed!

The human race has also been influenced by popular culture: books, plays and, more recently, TV and films. The movie *Ghost*, the 1990 film starring Patrick

Swayze, Demi Moore and Whoopi Goldberg, was particularly persuasive with its view of Sam, Patrick's character, disappearing up into a bright spotlight before fading gradually away as he headed up to heaven. Past times also had their fair share of afterlife 'experts', as we shall see.

The Poet Dante

Dante Alighieri wrote the *Divine Comedy*, an 'epic poem', in which he described what he felt heaven and hell might look like. He incorporated the visions of many cultural beliefs on the afterlife, including the Christian view of heaven and hell. Very simply, the work is split into three parts, 'Inferno', 'Purgatorio' and 'Paradiso'. Part one relates to humankind awakening to sin (lust, greed, etc.) and getting lost along life's path. Part two expresses the life of a Christian stepping out of 'hell' to the mountain of purgatory, and part three explains Dante's vision of the nine celestial spheres of heaven.

Dante's work in turn influenced many minds which came after (including artists and authors) about what a real afterlife might be like. His poem, composed of 14,233 lines that are divided into the three 'canticas', was written sometime between 1308 and his death in 1321.

Artist Michelangelo was one of the people swayed by his work; his fresco *Last Judgement* (in the Sistine Chapel) portrays a heaven and hell. This in turn influenced Western culture's view of the other side.

Our Vision of Heaven

The online encyclopaedia Wikipedia describes the seven heavens as a common religious or metaphysical term for a place where God, angels and spirits reside after physical death. It's called both a paradise and a higher place, or the 'holiest' place, in contrast to hell, which is called the 'low' place.

Heaven is often viewed as a 'place' which seems to get further away as our scientific knowledge grows; for example, a hundred years ago, heaven was thought to be right above our heads. Once humankind mastered aeroplanes, and heaven still wasn't to be found, heaven became a place that was outside of our atmosphere. Now we are space beings, heaven is considered to be a place outside of our galaxy! To be honest, the 'higher vibration' theory, of heaven being all around us, now makes the most sense of all.

Many of us confuse heaven with something they might have seen in an old black-and-white movie. Do we still believe heaven to be a place where we sit on clouds all day playing harps? Children at least view heaven as a place with no pain or suffering, a perfect place of existence . . . they may be right if modern-day accounts have anything to do with it. Is heaven our final resting place or just somewhere we call home that we visit on our way to other places . . . or spaces?

Is heaven an actual place or is it a state of being? We understand that it is somewhere without time, time being an earthly concept. The problem is that as humans we need to compare everything with what we have here on earth and everything that we currently understand. Maybe that is why so many people do actually see beautiful gardens and crystal buildings!

Heaven is thought to be a place of perfect supernatural happiness, a space of peace and total unconditional love. Our deceased loved ones and pets live in this happy place – many have seen them on brief visits to the other world. Our earthly lives do seem to dictate our experience of heaven at the point of near death or death. As the time draws near to the end of life, some people begin to have visions and visits from the deceased, as we've already discovered. Amongst the visitors are deceased loved ones, pets, angels and guides. One thing is sure, since the beginning of time, people have been searching for heaven in the same way that they have been looking for the meaning of life. It's one of humankind's biggest questions. Maybe we will never know the total truth but we do have so many clues. It's exciting picking up the pieces and creating a partially finished jigsaw!

Heaven has been called Utopia, Shangri-La and Nirvana. Other cultures call heaven the happy hunting grounds and even paradise lost (also the name of another epic poem, this time by seventeenth-century English poet John Milton). History suggests that searching for heaven in this world is like searching for an illusion. Religions can help us to make sense of God, but whether they give us all the answers about heaven is up to you to decide. Some believe that heaven is a place we hold in our hearts or a place we can visit through dreams, prayer and meditation.

Throughout history religious figures like Buddha and Jesus have helped us to understand the concept that heaven can be found within ourselves and that love is the way to heaven. Heaven is an experiential place rather than a physical place . . . although, strangely, people see a physical place when they go there!

Some Thoughts on 'Hell'

Often when you hear the word heaven, you may hear the word hell mentioned in the same sentence, but is hell really an actual place or a state of being? Does it even exist at all? This is something I wanted to find out more about and so did some lengthy research. What was shocking to me the most is that hell, as described in my English bible, may actually be a description which occurs due to mistakes in translation! So is hell not the place of purgatory, fire and damnation that we have read about? Have we got it wrong for hundreds of years?

During my research I discovered that if we examine the source words that are translated as 'hell' in the various editions of the English-language bibles, the original meaning becomes clearer. The word 'hell' is actually translated from several different Greek and Hebrew words. In the original languages, the words are not interchangeable, yet bizarrely, in English-language bibles, the words have been translated differently in different parts of the bible. Maybe this was due in part to the beliefs of the translators themselves (rather than any intent to deceive). The translators used words which they felt gave the best meaning rather than the words that were originally intended. Consistency is not even present and the same words have been translated with different meanings in different places. It's confusing, right?

Gehennah is one word translated as 'hell' in the bible, although the Jews knew it as a physical place. Gehennah is a valley located to the south of Jerusalem. In Hebrew it means 'valley of the sons of Hennah'. Once upon a time, child sacrifices were made to the pagan god Moloch at this place – certainly a hellish place but not the hell of the bible, surely? Many years later, after the place came under Jewish control, a memorial fire was kept burning on the spot and later still the whole area became a dumping ground for rubbish, and even the bodies of the poor who could not afford a proper burial. In an attempt to keep the place sanitary, fires of the remains and rubbish burnt continuously. It became known as a kind of allegory of a place where the doomed or worst members of society might end up after death as a sort of punishment, but are we talking of the resting place of the physical body or the spirit?

In the Old Testament, the word 'punish' is translated from ten different Hebrew words, none of which mean 'punish' in the English language. The word *paqad* really means to remember or to visit. Another word, *anash*, actually means to push for or coerce. Rather than mean hell, the word *chasak*, which occurs three times, simply means to restrain, and so on. These translations seem to suggest that every time God simply visits someone, he is punishing them, which is clearly not the case. An interesting topic for debate, I'm sure!

> 'It is better to conquer yourself than to win a
> thousand battles. Then the victory is yours.
> It cannot be taken from you, not by angels or
> by demons, heaven or hell.'
> Buddha

I am by no means an expert on the biblical translations (I know very little about it, to be honest), but I did stray across some very interesting information when doing my research. For example, in the Gospel story of Lazarus and the Rich Man, Jesus says that they both end up in the same place, in Hades. Hades, of course, is used to mean the same thing as the Hebrew word *Sheol*, it simply means the place everyone goes when they die; yet the word 'Hades' is translated over and over again as 'hell' in the New Testament! It's fascinating, but ultimately we all have to make up our own minds what we believe.

Another interesting discovery was that the Greek word for 'divine' (or 'divine being') also means sulphur or the old English word 'brimstone' – a burning stone! You can see where the confusion might occur here, right? The word *theion* is translated as 'brimstone' – a word interchangeable with the words 'divine fire' (or 'divine light'), and not really meaning a hellish place at all.

Incidentally, the Old English word 'hell' comes from the word *helan*, which means 'to cover or hide from' (it's a verb). To be in hell then indicates being hidden or covered, not seeing God or not being in God's space or divine light. The poet Dante (in his *Inferno*) 'corrupted' the use of the word in the middle ages; it became a noun through common use and as his work was so popular, the concept became ingrained into common thought . . . hence 'hell' becomes a place of fire and brimstone, an actual place where the bad are taken or find themselves at the point of death.

In reality then, hell is not a place but a condition or state of being. If we turn from God's love, our condition becomes hellish, meaning we are away from the light of our creator. Hell seems not to be a place of punishment for wrongdoings on earth, and certainly heaven or the condition of 'hell' is so faced as a result of our own self-judgement. We punish ourselves and create a mental state of 'hell'.

> 'Heaven means to be one with God.'
> Confucius

At the point of leaving the body (as in a near-death experience), some find themselves witnessing their entire life 'pass before their eyes' as part of a whole series of phenomena which occurs after death. The spirit will view the life lived so far in the body of the human – their actions, their reactions, and everything they've said and done is recalled somehow. (We looked at this earlier, if you remember.) In reviewing their life the 'deceased' will in part re-live certain aspects of their life, especially those parts where they helped or hurt others, and the repercussions of those experiences. For example, if you said something mean to another child at pre-school you would feel their hurt and then experience the pain as that child went on to kick another child in anger as a result of the unkind words that you spoke to them.

Every action, word and deed on our part has a consequence . . . and we get to see this at the point of death. I imagine that in itself is 'hell', but only one of our own making. Those experiencing near death usually return to life saying that they felt the only person judging them was themselves. The torment is only within ourselves.

Heaven can be seen partly as a state of nearness to God; hell is a state of remoteness, or a state of being hidden from God – but, remember, a remoteness of our own making or choice!

That's a little deep, isn't it, but remember these are just my own musings based on the little research I have done, so take from this what feels right to you and, if you want to, go and do a little more research for yourself. I think it's fairly safe to say that hell, as it's portrayed as a place of fire and brimstone, probably doesn't exist, so I wouldn't worry too much about it!

Now, let's have a look at how some others have viewed heaven from around the world.

Views of Heaven

Ancient Greece

According to the ancient Greeks, after death you would be taken to a place known as Hades, which was governed by the god of the same name. It may have been helpful to have a sack of provisions with you as you had to please a lot of people along the way. Your journey would take you across the river Styx (so you'd need a coin for Charon, the boatman). Next you'd be expected to feed Cerberus, the dog with three heads. He had a preference for honey cake apparently!

The ancient Greeks had a vision of an Underworld in which the bad were punished and the good were offered pleasure. A beautiful, sunlight green paradise known as the Elysian Fields was the final resting place for those that had lived a good life.

Ancient Rome

Several views were prevalent during these times: one suggested that life on earth was seen as a type of prison before the spirit earned the right to release itself into the Milky Way. So death was viewed as life, and life was the death of the soul.

At the same time, it was wrong to wish to speed up death; and a life of good deeds and honour was needed to guarantee a joyous afterlife.

Australian Aborigines

The world of spirit and the physical world are closely connected. The end of bodily life means that the spirit is free to join one's ancestors in the 'Dreamtime'. Some, but not all tribes, hold the belief that the spirit can choose to be born again.

The Aztecs

The dead were expected to undertake a challenging journey following their passing from one life to the next, encountering treacherous landscapes and dangerous creatures. A man's dog would be sacrificed at his owner's passing so that the two of them could cross the 'Ninefold Stream' to finally enter the Chicomemictlan, or 'house of the dead', together.

Ancient Egypt

The Ancient Egyptians' beliefs are well recorded, with many Egyptians spending their lives preparing for their deaths. The rich Pharaohs created fancy tombs and built up food stocks to be buried alongside their servants, whose lives were also sacrificed at the death of their masters.

Bodies were preserved intact (often by being mummified, a costly procedure) and food offerings were presented to the body after death. The soul was believed to be judged by the gods Horus and Thoth in the Hall of Maat. The soul was weighed against a feather (the weighing of the heart). 'Heavy hearts' were swallowed by the Devourer of Souls and the good souls were sent to the 'Happy Fields' to be with the god of the underworld (Osiris). Suggestions, ideas and spells for reaching these higher realms rather than being devoured were recorded in the Book of the Dead.

Polynesia (Maoris, New Zealand)

The afterlife is also seen here as a journey that involves crossing over a river. The deceased expect to meet up with loved ones who have previously passed on. The path to the afterlife is expected to be dangerous, with challenges such as monsters and difficult terrain along the way! In some cases it is possible to travel back from the dead, as long as one doesn't eat anything once you reach the other side.

Hinduism

In Hinduism the life goal is to escape the continuous circle of birth, death and rebirth after which Hindus would expect to go to an eternal resting place in the arms of a loving God by way of one of four paths: Jnana yoga is the path of knowledge; Bhakti yoga, the path of love (salvation through worship of a divine being); Karma yoga, the way of action through good works; and Raja yoga, known as the royal road, which uses meditative yoga techniques.

Islam

The Koran (the Islamic holy book) explains that salvation depends on a person's actions and attitudes throughout their life. Repentance can save you, though. On the final day of reckoning every man has to account for his actions and deeds and his afterlife will be decided based upon these, although individual situations are taken into account. The Koran describes both a heaven and hell.

Buddhism

The original Buddhist teaching puts emphasis on an individual working through self-controlled meditative practices which eventually lead him to the state of Nirvana. Nivana means 'blowing out', in the way you would blow out a candle flame. It is also explained or likened to the unfolding petals of a lotus flower.

Tibetan Buddhism

The Shaman, or wise man, is expected to guide souls on the right path. Like the Egyptians, the Tibetans' also have a Book of the Dead (the *Bardo Thodol*), which records information to guide the dying. The body is expected to witness many false demons on its journey back to life.

The State of Being Relating to Suicide

People sometimes write and ask me about what happens to the souls of those who 'cross themselves over' (take their own lives). Just as with the other information I have gathered over the years, my views here come from numerous sources, including those who have experienced near death from attempting to take their own lives, stories of visits from the other side and people who have past-life recall (spontaneously or using deep hypnotic trance) amongst others.

The simple answer is that those who take their own lives almost always immediately regret that they have done so. There is no judgement (not from souls/angels on the other side, as we have already seen), but they will experience the sadness and loss of those on this side of life, the people they leave behind. Strangely, just when you feel that life is no longer worth living, or you feel that no one loves you, this is when you understand that, actually, you were important to so many people that you had not even begun to realize! You will be missed and people are sad; you feel their loss and experience the repercussions of your decision to end your own life. It's really rather heart-breaking.

When we choose our lives before birth, we also agree to interact with many others along the way. Imagine how your life might help these people as the years pass by. If you are no longer on earth because you have chosen to end your life before your time, your role in these important events in other people's lives can no longer take place. In effect, you have broken your life-contract with these people, your agreement with other souls (many even strangers to you in this lifetime at this point).

Let's look at some examples of what I mean by this. During your life you effect/help many people in ways that you can't even begin to imagine:

- One day you smile at a stranger in the street.
  Maybe that person lost a loved one that very day

and you give them the strength to carry on with their own life? You'll probably never even know how you've helped.

- Perhaps you give some words of advice to a stranger whilst waiting in a queue; those words of advice change that person's life forever in a positive way, though you never discover the outcome.
- A dog runs into the road and you manage to grab the lead before a car swerves to avoid it . . . perhaps several people might have been hurt or fatally injured? Because you stopped it happening, the people were safe but you had no idea that the outcome could have been so bad if you hadn't been there.
- You give a neighbour a lift in your car – if she had walked to work on that very day, she may have missed an important job interview at a place where she was meant to meet her future husband.

Of course, these are just made-up scenarios but what I am saying is that your life – your future life – is not just about you, but about how you connect with and help others, and all of these things will have been agreed before birth. Small things you do today can have a widespread effect. Each little act of kindness spreads out like ripples on a pond. Many religions have rules which forbid the taking of your own life . . . for very good reasons.

People take their own lives for many reasons: fear, threat,

distress, grief, depression, illness, etc. Often their hope is that the pain will end upon death and that they will be with those that have passed before in a non-physical way. My postbag reflects that the reality is often a little different.

I've had numerous letters from people over the years who have attempted to take their own life and right away realized that they had made a mistake, but the judgement comes not from others but from themselves. The future is nearly always brighter in a way they could never have imagined. Passing from suicide can mean a time of confusion on the other side. This is where the sense of 'hell' comes from, hell in the sense of being detached from the light. The sadness and loss can carry on for a while (and although help is always available in the afterlife, we might not immediately see or seek it).

I did have a real think about whether or not to include this story but felt that, to be fair, I should give you an example (a rare example) of how this might play out. This story is a visitation, but not the happy, comforting type of story that usually reaches my postbag (I have removed the names here for privacy).

Sorrow

I dreamt I was in a dark empty room; the room was quite big. The only furniture in the room was chairs (like the ones from a dining table). I was sitting on one of the chairs and to my left was a girl who had taken her own life. I recognized her. I didn't know her in real life but my friends did, and they'd all gone to her funeral. Sadly, this young woman had hung herself and had left behind a five-year-old daughter.

I spoke to her but she didn't reply. Her eyes were filled with tears and I could feel her sorrow; she was just staring at me.

When we use the phrase 'may their soul rest in peace', or 'I hope they are at peace now', what we mean is, we hope their torment has ended. It's like a built-in understanding that death is NOT the answer to solve all problems . . . or even any of them. We wish the soul of the deceased a happy release now they are in their new space/life.

What I have discovered is that prayers and love sent to those who have taken their own lives, messages and best wishes, do help the deceased, and we can reach them in this way. Ultimately there appears to be lots of help for souls in distress for whatever reason, angels and guides whose role it is to comfort and support those that have passed. Do not worry if you know someone who has crossed at their own hands. Their confusion and worry does not go on forever. When they are ready, help is waiting for them. Forgiving yourself as a soul seems to be the most important step for the newly passed, whatever the reason.

Here is another reader's story.

Heartbreak Hotel

I met a man who was younger than me and we got together. It didn't work out so I ended the relationship and the man, whom I won't name, took it really badly. Ultimately he took his own life. It was completely shocking, especially as he left a letter saying that he couldn't live without me.

I can't even begin to explain how I felt after it happened and it really messed me up. I had to go on medication because I was so upset that he'd taken his life over me. I couldn't seem to move on and eventually I decided that the best way to deal with the situation was for me to take my own life too. I saved up my medication so that I could do this and then one afternoon I went to lie on the bed with that very thought in my head. After that I simply don't know what happened to me; I just felt myself being drawn up from the bed through a tunnel, and at the end of the tunnel was a very bright blue light. I could make out the outline of a person at the end by the light and then I heard a man's voice tell me that I had to go back because it wasn't my time! I could feel this deep sense of peace, it was such a lovely feeling, and then I could hear Elvis Presley singing 'Heartbreak Hotel'.

Next I remember thinking about my little dog who was only two years old. Who would look after her if I was no longer there? At this point I seemed to become aware of my surroundings again, but the strangest thing was that on the floor by the side of my bed was a magazine with an article about the song 'Heartbreak Hotel'. It explained how the lyrics had been written about a young boy who'd committed suicide. I sat and read the article and afterwards the magazine just seemed to have vanished. I never found it again.

I'm fifty-six now and since this time I've started to read more about angels. I really believe that someone was looking after me that day.

Linda, Wales

None of us has walked in another's shoes, or lived their lives; none of us – living or deceased – can pass sentence on another. Ultimately life can be fun, exciting, breathless and loving, and many other things including challenging! We all do the best we can at any given time. Like many families, we too have a family member that 'crossed themselves over'. Many years after her death she visited us from the other side. She was, she said, finally 'at peace'.

If you're depressed or thoughts of 'crossing yourself over' have passed your mind then do seek help from your doctor. It's not a normal feeling to want to take your own life – the mind naturally protects life at all costs. It may be simply that you are suffering from depression and the solution might be counselling or medication of some sort. Please, for me, make sure you explore every opportunity here on earth. Let your doctor help you. Once on suitable medication you will likely feel completely different and be so relieved that you didn't take the next step.

This section is based on the experience and knowledge I have gained from the work I have done. It's a difficult subject to cover, even for a professional, but it was harder still to leave it out from a book about heaven because it comes up occasionally in my postbag. In no way is it meant to be an explanation of exactly what happens in every case. If a person is near death and in pain, for example, the scenario is, of course, quite different (maybe modern medicine means that a person is living longer than was intended for their body). If this information feels right to you then that is great, but if you are not comfortable with viewing loss in this way then it's OK to ignore what I have suggested above. You may be more comforted by explanations from your religion or family teachings and, of course, that is completely fine. Please feel free to disregard anything in this section (in the whole book, in fact) which does not feel right to you.

Our whole view of heaven, hell and other such sensitive issues is very personal. I guess, as I have suggested earlier, my own views and experience will inevitably influence the words I have shared in this book!

A Child's Point of View: What is Heaven?

Lastly, I thought it would be fun – and apt – to ask some children what their own thoughts were on heaven; after all, if you look at it logically, children have only recently been born from that very place, so they should know, shouldn't they? It's definitely time for a little 'light relief' after this very 'challenging' chapter!

These stories all come from fans on my Facebook page (and thank you to everyone who helped with this section).

Here are my favourite replies in answer to the question: 'What is heaven?'

Andrea – 'Leo, age six, said, "It's a big wonderland that's in space with really good things and it's in your imagination and love goes up there . . ."'

Amanda – 'When my daughter Jade was about seven she asked about heaven and I tried my best to explain to her; she pondered what I had said about doing good deeds and having good morals, etc. She came back and said, "Does that mean that we'll be eating chocolate and naughty people will be sweeping the streets?" . . . Such a simple view!'

Rachel – 'Katie, age three, said, "It's where the angels play." Lizzie, age twelve, said, "It's whatever you want it to be, so in your case, Mum, it's covered in chocolate!"'

Emma – 'Ethan, age four, said, "Where you go when you die, Mufasa [from *The Lion King*] and Auntie Janet are there . . ."'

Shelly – 'Ryan, age eight, says, "It's a place where angels live who look after our loved ones, and where we all will live one day."'

Andrea – 'Me and my son spoke about this yesterday. He said, "It's in each and every one of us, it's whatever the individual wants it to be." Kyle is nineteen, not so young, but I loved his reasoning.'

Sara – 'Kenzie, age four, said, "Heaven is a world in the sky where my nana and grandad are and other dead people."'

Tia – 'Me, age ten: "I think heaven is what you make of it, if you want it to be paradise it is. We decide."'

Alexandra – 'Connor, age twelve: "Living here."'

Suzanne – 'My son Andrew, age eleven, said that Heaven was a place where the righteous and those who have repented go, to be with God, the angels, saints, the apostles and all those who have passed away.'

Lorna – 'Paris, age seven, said, "I think heaven is a place of happiness and angels, with lots of dogs to play with the angels. I think it's bright coloured with lots of rainbows; God and Jesus are there and other people that have died. Nobody is nasty, only kind people, and people read books, help each other and walk the dogs for their old owners." Very detailed.'

Tanya – 'Lucy, aged six, said, "When you die you go up into heaven; it's a very nice place where you see friends and family again."'

Michelle – 'My son Adam, age seventeen, said, "It's a happy place and will be pain free . . . and how you want it to be."'

Helen – 'I asked my eleven-year-old and he said, "Big white fluffy clouds and it's really bright and white. God and Jesus live there and dead people but they can't see their feet!"'

Jayne – 'My son Scott, age nine, said, "I know there are angels in heaven!"'

Tanya: – 'Luke, age seven, said, "It's where dead people go," bless him.'

Lisa – 'My daughter Gracie, age eight, once said, "Heaven is God's most beautiful garden; it has the brightest rainbows and flowers and everyone loves one another there. If you're really good, you get to eat all the nicest cakes too."'

Penny – 'Charlotte, age six (who is autistic), said, "A place where Nanny is," followed by, "How do I know? I'm not dead!"'

Val – 'I asked two of my daughters, Katie, age eight, and Kerry, age seven. They both said heaven is up, it's where God lives and when people die they go up to heaven.'

Sabrina – 'Tammy, age eight, said, "It's where my daddy went before I was born and now he's an angel."

'William died ten weeks before Tammy was born. I woke to find him dead beside me. I was frantic. The love of my life had suddenly passed away. When Tammy was born the labour was only twenty-two minutes long! William was at work in such a short time making the labour pain free. I didn't see him but I felt his presence and that helped the grieving too, as well as the beautiful daughter I have today.'

James – 'My daughter Carra, age twelve, said, "It's whatever you want it to be."'

Nona – 'Lauren, age nine, said, "When people and pets die, their soul floats up to heaven; it's a big sheet of clouds for the floor. There are different floors; the souls go to different floors. There is a separate cloud where pets are." Joshua, age six, said, "It's a place where people go when they die . . . and their pets."'

Jayne – 'My daughter Lauren, age eleven, said, "It's where Hollie [our boxer dog] is playing fetch with Grandma, and Grandad is making sure that all the beautiful flowers are watered every day."'

Rachael – 'Rosie, age six, said, "Where angels live."'

Gaynor – 'My granddaughter Ashleigh, age ten, said, "It's a place where spirits go to rest in peace."'

Nicola – 'Zak, age four, said, "Where flowers, children and angels are."'

Debstar – 'Mitchell, age five, said, "It's where we go when we die to be with God and the fairies . . . and with Rocky [our cat that passed away last year]. Oh yeah, and that little boy that Nanny saw in the house!"'

Jo – 'Marrisa, age four, said, "Where you go up in the sky to go to bed and sleep until the stars come out and look after us."'

Nadia-Salvatore – 'Angelo, age seven, said, "It's a world where you could wish for anything you wanted and what you sit on is cloud."'

Carrie-Ann – 'Cameron, age seven, said, "When people die that's where their ghosts live and they can come down and talk to you. That's what heaven is, isn't it?"'

Laura Louise – 'Chelsea Johnson, age eight, said, "Where people who are dead go to live up there and they fly up there."'

Sandra – 'Lucia, age thirteen, said, "Happiness, cheerful and where dead people go!"'

Michelle – 'My daughter Eva-Marie, age five, said, "It's a place you go when you die." However, she also believes that her Gran Jessie went to live on the sun when she passed over and her papa Derek went to live on the moon when he passed over; they are there to watch over us and look after us.'

James – 'My other daughter, Mia, age six, said, "It's a place you go when you die and they look after them there."'

Angelina – 'Our oldest daughter, Erin, age eleven, says, "Heaven is somewhere you are happy to be in, like being at home. Home is heaven."'

Tracy – 'My ten-year-old, James, says, "It's a place for people to go when they die," and my seven-year-old, Heather, says, "It's a place for hamsters to go to . . . and the people can visit them."'

Angela – 'I just asked my daughter, Ellie-Marie, age nine. She said, "It's a lovely place in the clouds where my other family live, they come back sometimes for a quick visit but then go back because they like it better . . . oh and God's there."'

Chantal – 'Dominique, age eleven, said, "A place for angels and people that were good on earth."'

Shamiema – 'Nabeel, ten years old, said, "It's a place in the sky, where the people we love go when they die, and at night when it's dark, those people that we love come down and plant kisses on our foreheads when we are asleep."'

Kerry – 'My youngest daughter, Daisy (who is autistic), age twelve, said, "It is paradise for the good people. It is very white as snow and full of angels."'

Michelle – 'Joe, age three, said, "There are like rockets there that can fly to the moon and they look down on us when we are sleeping."'

Angelina – 'My youngest daughter, Teagan, age six, said, "Heaven is the place you go to when you are dead, the angels are there and they play with you."'

Laura – 'Lauren, age seven, said, "Heaven is a place you go when you are dead; up in the sky with Toby [our pet Labrador]."'

Hilary – 'Melissa, age twelve, said heaven is a "big magical place with clouds where everything is happy and right".'

Sarah – 'Ben, age ten, who has Asperger's Syndrome, said, "Well, you did ask . . . Heaven is where you die, it's underground and it's very dirty."'

Sarah – 'Ruby, age six, said, "Heaven is something that is good, but some people might find it a bit bad. You go there when you die."'

Jayne – 'My daughter Emma, age eleven, said, "If you've been good, it's where your spirit goes and meets God 'n' Jesus."'

Jennifer – 'Tamara, age five, said heaven is "a place where, if you're good, you can have lollies every day".'

Doris – 'Josh, age seven, said, "Where the angels take you when it's your time, and to watch over you."'

Shimmer – 'My daughter Aoibheann, age four, said, "It's where peoples go when they die and God and Mary is in there." Then she said, "Aw . . . I know the baby Jesus is in there too!"'

I think you'll agree that children are very wise indeed. I don't think I could have explained heaven any better myself if I'd tried!

Right . . . now to answer some of your many questions about the life hereafter. It's a big section and if you've ever wondered about something relating to what happens next, there is a fair chance I've come across the question before. The great thing is that I've received so many of your stories over the years, I have been able to share some of the answers I've learnt from them – and it's fascinating stuff!

Read on . . .

Questions About the Afterlife

'The chief problem about death, incidentally,
is the fear that there may be no afterlife;
a depressing thought, particularly for those
who have bothered to shave.'

Woody Allen

Here are some of the most regularly asked questions from my postbag; some of these questions are from my Facebook followers. My answers are formulated from a lifetime of studying the phenomena and my information comes from various sources, including personal experiences, real-life experiences from my postbag from those who have encountered the afterlife or had deceased loved ones visit with information, hundreds of books on psychic and paranormal phenomena relating to life and the afterlife, and many more. The questions – and the answers too, I think you'll find – are fascinating!

Some questions I have chosen to put together because they are very similar.

Are afterlife experiences real?
Near-death-experience expert Dr Bruce Greyson (psychiatrist at the University of Virginia), after having studied

more than 100 cases on incidents of near death, believes that near-death experiences suggest the mind functions outside of the physical body.

Is this a common phenomenon?
According to one survey, 65 per cent of widows and widowers report encounters with their departed spouses (so more do than don't). Looking at the number of books now written on this subject (including many of my own books on afterlife events), then I would have to say *yes*. Many, many people of all ages, races, sexes and backgrounds are having contact from their loved ones in the afterlife. The facts indicate that the afterlife – heaven – is real. My files (and books) are full of real-life encounters with the other side.

What happens to the soul once the body dies? Where does it go?
Neurosurgeon Dr Eben Alexander III (associate professor at Harvard Medical School) had a type of near-death experience in 2008, after contracting a rare form of bacterial meningitis. He was almost brain dead for seven days. Alexander recalls a journey through 'the core' whilst in his coma and came face to face with the vision of God. After his recovery he knew without a doubt that there was another existence beyond this one.

Millions of people have experienced 'near death' (that is, they died but were then brought back to life again). This is one of the many ways we know what comes next on our spiritual journey. Remember that 'death' as we know it is just a rebirth in another form. We've been through this experience many times before and we'll be doing it many more times in the future.

Does our life on earth and our experience and beliefs here on earth affect the next part of the journey?
Not necessarily. My research shows that it can at first, i.e. if you expect to see a certain person on the other side after you pass over, or expect to be at a particular place, then your experience may well reflect your expectation . . . initially. If you believed there was no heaven when you were alive then you might not find anything at first (and are less likely to contact the living because you assume you can't).

All these things can change though; even people who expect to end up in a dark place (and remember they might, initially), can 'look to the light' quite literally, forgive themselves and raise their vibration to find themselves in a higher, more loving environment, heaven. Live your life on earth as you would like to be perceived in heaven. The key to a positive afterlife seems to be to live a positive life, especially to love unselfishly . . . it's never too late to change your ways!

Are our loved ones OK? Did they make it safely to heaven?
In most cases, yes; even if you don't get a sign, your loved ones are probably completely fine. Not everyone is able to communicate from the other side and not everyone is able to receive a message, even if they can. You mustn't

worry either way. Even if there is an issue, spirits (sometimes even deceased loved ones) are placed in charge of caring for those in the afterlife until they become aware and awakened. Your loved one will be taken care of.

If they've suffered physically on earth, are our loved ones well now?

Yes, many of the stories in my files over the years seem to indicate that after passing on, a healing process can take place in the afterlife. In some cases this is brief and in other cases it may take many months or years to complete.

Physical ailments disappear once our loved ones are on the other side of life; after all, once we shed our physical bodies we have no need of carrying our illnesses on to our spiritual bodies, our soul. Sometimes our deceased loved ones will appear to the living carrying (at least initially) their previous sickness or disorder as a way of identifying themselves. For example, my late father appeared to his grandchildren complete with his glasses and walking stick (neither of which he needed in heaven!). The grandchildren were grateful that Grandad still looked like Grandad!

What about healing for the people who have died in tragic circumstances and suicides, what happens?

After my aunt passed away, my father appeared in a dream to my sister to explain that she would be unable to visit us any time soon because she was being healed on the other side. She did eventually visit me in a dream after about a year. This is a common phenomenon and when the living interact with the deceased during dream visitations, asking why they didn't visit earlier, this is one of the reasons they give.

How does this healing take place?
In many ways. Some find themselves in a healing chamber or healing tube after crossing over; others wake in a type of hospital setting (a reference to a familiar healing place here on earth). Others go through a type of healing light or shower. This can take as long as the soul wishes. This can also happen during a near-death experience, especially if someone has been unconscious for a long time following some type of illness or accident. A person might be in a coma on the earth plane but their soul spends time in a heavenly healing chamber (and, believe it or not, some people remember this happening!).

Can they see what I'm doing on this side of life? Do they know I finally passed my test/got married/ recovered from my accident?
It seems that they can. Many folk report dream visits or pick up signs during important occasions. The deceased can even appear in photographs taken at the time of a special family celebration. They can tune in to our lives when there is a desire to do so on both sides (we both wish it); they usually do this so that they can keep up to date with our progress here on earth . . . rather than spying on us! (It has to come from a vibration of love.)

Do they still love us? Are they proud of me?
Of course! Love never dies and if they choose to follow along with your earthly lives, as many do, they will be proud of you now as they would have been had they lived – if not more so, as they are more aware of the circumstances surrounding our achievements and the challenges we've had to deal with along the way.

Will I see them again?
Yes. When it's 'your time', those that we loved the most on earth are the ones that are there to meet us when we cross over. If there were close family members that you didn't get on with or people that harmed you (physically or mentally) in life, they won't be in the welcome committee . . . it's just not allowed.

How do I know they're OK?
They are! Sometimes they are able to pop back and bring a sign, but if they don't, know that they are being taken care of in heaven and there is nothing for you to worry about at all. As my dad once explained, 'We have lives in heaven too!'

What is my loved one doing now?
Good question. Any number of things . . . Whatever they wish, is the best answer I can give. My research suggests that the deceased have full and active lives on heaven-side; and this information comes from numerous sources over many years. Bear with me, as I know this sounds weird.

They have indicated that they have great freedom to continue to study and grow. Their lives might include:

- Looking back on their past life to see how they got on and how they might improve next life around.
- Helping new people to integrate on heaven-side.
- Acting as guides to those on earth.
- Helping those in physical bodies to 'cross over' when it's their time.
- Creating/manifesting things/building . . . helping to grow some of those beautiful green parks people talk about.
- Teaching.
- Attending classes.
- Creating harmony (playing music, mixing colours), for heaven, earth and other realms and planets.
- Leisure and having fun/interacting with other souls (especially their soul group – those they have spent this life and other lives with).
- Continuing research into things that interested them in life (or other lives).
- Planning their next life.

My late uncle once came back to tell me he was 'messing around' on the other side! He was a funny man in life too but then spent many years guiding me on this side, so his new existence included an important role as well as having fun.

I remember one visitation story in which a deceased

family member came to visit a relative of mine. He told my relative that he had a lot of fun now 'flying' in heaven. Now, wouldn't you like to have a go at that? I know I would.

How do they contact us and what can I do to help instigate the phenomenon in my own life? I've heard it can take a loved one time to settle before they can make contact, if they chose to do so. Is this true? This question has quite a long answer really but we can invite them to make contact and if they are able they will certainly try.

- Reaching out to earth-side takes enormous effort and energy on both sides. We know that many deceased souls that do come back are usually accompanied by an angel or guide who help provide additional support for this endeavour. At other times the deceased is assisted by other deceased loved ones to help create more 'energy' to enable the contact to take place.
- Some souls seem to specialize in reaching out, as if they have spent time learning the skill.
- Being open to receiving contact, requesting it or anticipating it, can help. Many have contact from the other side after talking about the phenomenon with friends or reading up on the subject. Our earthly interest seems to help draw the phenomenon towards us.
- Being fearful or saying things like, 'I'd be scared if Mum came to visit me,' seem to be reasons

why the visitation might not happen. There is a universal law which suggests that the visit may take place if it helps the grieving but not if it harms or makes life more difficult or depressing. We need to be emotionally 'ready' for the contact.

- The request has to be granted, i.e. some people say their deceased loved ones come back and say things like, 'God gave me permission to come back one last time and say goodbye.'

- You can also visit a psychic medium, of course (an intermediary between heaven and earth), but results are not guaranteed; it depends on the skill of the medium or the wish of the spirit to connect. There are other things you can do if you wish (and with an expert) – hold a seance, for example.

- In my experience, the most successful communications seem to be when the deceased simply bring a sign that they are around (like a white feather) or appear to you in a dream visit. Try simply asking for one and see how you get on.

I'm just fascinated and curious – what is heaven like?
Well, that's another great question! Heaven is a vast place with many layers and tiers of vibration. When we pass on we are drawn to the right level where we belong (like being pulled along in a slipstream or river), to the place which is most like that of our own vibration (spiritual progression). We can't get lost.

218

The lower levels (those closest to the earth) are the slowest/less spiritually developed but these can also be an entry or border-crossing type of place where we settle at first until we are ready to move up to our correct 'space'. I think of it as a hotel near the airport!

These slower spaces are the most like earth but people consistently say that everything is brighter, cleaner, more 'sparkling' and more beautiful than earth. There are buildings, parks, rivers and oceans like on earth but the rules are different. You can't drown in the rivers; you won't want to pick the flowers because they are beautiful where they are (and have a more alive type of life force, a life energy that earth flowers don't); and you don't 'own' things in the way you do on earth.

As you move up through the higher realms you shed your need for earth-like surroundings and you too become finer and of a lighter substance. We know much less about the very highest realms as the more spiritual beings who reside in this space are less likely to reincarnate back on earth to tell us about it! The highest (more loving) vibration is closer to God/the source/our creator.

Can my loved ones see me all the time or just when they choose to? And do they hear the things we say to them when we talk to them in spirit?
Well, they don't hang around all day watching what we do, if that's what you mean. When we think of them (or talk about them), they are aware of it and can tune in at that time if they wish. If we talk to them then they can

hear what we say (I often get stories from relatives who want to share coincidence-type experiences that show the deceased really do hear what we say).

What happens when you cross over in the moment you get there?
This information forms the near-death experience and a whole list of phenomena occurs. This can include some or all of the following:

- Seeing a tunnel of light.
- Being met by angels, guides or deceased loved ones.
- Finding soulmates (our soul group), which is made up of the closest groups of people we have incarnated with in this and other lives.
- Being met by deceased loved ones, friends, old neighbours, old work colleagues, etc. (those that had meaning for us during our lifetime).
- Seeing a life review (witnessing our life just lived).
- Going through a healing session.
- Orientation.

If you married more than once or have had more than one partner featuring in your life, and you loved both, who meets you when you pass over and who do you reside with in heaven? What happens when you have had two marriages? Which husband do you meet? Are there no bad feelings and you all harmon-

ize together? Will my late husband, if I meet him there, forgive me for getting married again? He was a very jealous person.

This reader has a lot of questions, but I have kept them all together here. The answer really is that if you loved both partners then both will meet you. If you loved one and not the other then the one who you loved will meet you. Of course, if you really didn't like either it's possible that neither will come!

In heaven, we are souls not humans. We are not male or female (although sometimes people keep their favourite gender in the level closest to the earth). So therefore the jealousy that we have as humans doesn't exist on the other side. Pure souls do not have gender so sexual jealousy does not exist.

Finally, in nearly every case, the deceased encourage us to marry again and form new relationships. The new partner may even be part of the same spiritual/soul group as you and your first husband! It's possible that you have all lived together in various ways in previous lifetimes (maybe last time you were the brother rather than the sister, or the daughter rather than the son, or whatever).

When we go back to spirit and meet people we knew on earth, will we recognize them?

Yes, we do. It's usual for us to be greeted by the deceased in the 'body' of their last life (the appearance of the body we recognize them in). If they appear in their spirit form (looking like a gaseous white cloud, for example), apparently we still know who they are!

Will they know how much they hurt us when they were here?

Oh, yes indeed. In fact, not only do they understand what they did to us, they also have to 'feel' the hurt they caused us (and any repercussions from their actions) as part of their past life review. Millions of people the world over have experienced seeing their 'life pass before their eyes' during near-death experiences. After seeing, feeling and experiencing the results of the actions they have performed in life (during the near-death experience), many people change the way they live when they come back, leaving relationships, moving house and retraining for different careers, etc.

Do they see us doing private things, for example, in the toilet, etc?

This always makes me laugh but I get asked this question such a lot. No, not really (although spirits do visit us in the bath and so on from time to time). They connect to us as spirit-to-spirit rather than spying on us during our private times in our naked bodies – it really doesn't work like that. Should you be lucky enough to be aware of a visit but it occurs at an inconvenient time, you can always ask them to leave.

Is there someone in heaven who judges whether we are worthy to be there? Or does everyone go there with a clean slate?

We looked at this question a little earlier in the book. During the 'review' of our life we do face a committee of sorts. Some people call these 'the wise ones' or 'the ancient ones' or similar. These 'people' (spirits) will be aware of the mistakes we have made but people have only described all their guides as being totally loving and non-judgemental. They often feel that they themselves are their only judge.

I wouldn't go so far as to say that we have a 'clean slate' because that would imply that we don't have to atone for the hurt we have done to others. We do have to atone, but not in the way you might imagine. If you kill someone during your lifetime, for example (even if it was accidental), your next life might include having to take care of that same soul, to 'balance the books'! It doesn't necessarily mean that the soul is going to kill you in your next life together! Rather than 'an-eye-for-an-eye', it's more like *If you damage my eyes then you have to take care of me when I go blind.*

Do we meet up with our deceased pets in heaven or do we never see them again?
We can meet up with them and we do. Pets often form part of the 'welcome home' committee, waiting to greet us as we pass into heaven. Deceased pets also visit us in dreams and so on after they have passed on themselves. Like humans, they also have souls (a different kind of soul) and they are aware – that awareness continues, along with the love we shared, after they pass on.

Do they still wear clothes like us? And, if so, do they get changed every day?
As spirits don't have bodies like us, then no, they don't really wear clothes. However, if they hold (form or create) a human body shape when they come to visit us, then they

can and do 'wear' clothes (or have the appearance of wearing clothes). Loved ones who visit in dream visitations from the afterlife will likely be 'wearing' their favourite clothes in heaven. They can also appear in floaty, ethereal gowns (as we might expect angels to wear!). I've never known a spirit appear to a human naked – but it could happen, I guess!

Why do some spirits choose to communicate with us after their passing and some don't?
We have covered this a little bit earlier in the book, but for clarification, here are some reasons again:

- They might not realize that they can visit earth again.
- Their earthly beliefs (maybe they didn't believe that the soul continued after death) or religious values may mean that they don't try.
- They don't have the spiritual strength to visit (it takes a lot of energy to do so but they can be helped by others on the other side).
- They may have tried but we missed the sign.
- We might not be receptive to their visit.
- Something about the way that we sleep (or filter information) might prevent them from communicating with us that way.
- They may be going through a healing type of experience.
- They may be spirits of a highly advanced nature that, after returning to heaven, go to a place

that makes it too difficult for them to reach down to our slower realms.

Do you believe there is a heaven and hell?
I believe there are different levels. Some people do see darker spaces when they pass over (because they expect to be punished), but my research shows that 'hell' is of our own creation, being a state of being where we are absent from the light of God. Those in higher realms are always reaching down to us, trying to raise us up, to literally 'look for the light'.

Some people say angels are your loved ones and others see them as the Victorian stereotypical wings and halo. How do you define what an angel is?
Well, during Victorian and earlier times, the mortality rate was much higher than it is today. Although women may have had many children, many less would live to adulthood. Grief was such that the belief that deceased loved ones became angels (especially the pure souls of babies) became stronger. If you look around old churches you can often see statues and carvings of babies with wings (cherubs, we call them).

People don't automatically become 'angels' when they pass but they do shed their bodies to become pure spirit once more . . . vibrating at the rate that they have spiritually attained. An angel is a being of 'light', something completely different, and the best way to describe this would be to say they were a different 'race' than human souls (in the way that a cat is not a dog, no matter what you do!).

If your soul is eternal, and you can live many lifetimes in order to learn your life lessons, do you just get to heaven when you have finally done that, and if so, how do you recognize your family/friends/partners when you have taken so many different forms? For example, I hope to meet my parents again in heaven, but if they had past lives, they may be someone else's parents too. Does that make sense?

Yes, your soul is eternal, but it doesn't matter which lives we have lived when we reconnect to loved ones on the other side. When they greet you they may appear initially as the parents you most recently knew but very soon you will recognize them as the old spirit friends you have connected with over and over in different lifetimes.

This gets complicated, but if we look at it in a very simple form, imagine that rather than greeting your mother, you are meeting the soul aspect – your 'mum' would be the larger 'hand' rather than the 'finger' (the most recent lifetime) you recognize her from. You know the hand, not just the fingers (which represent the individual lives).

I'm not sure that helped much! So let's just say, don't worry about it, you'll know who she is.

Do babies grow up in heaven or are they eternally babies?

Well, babies are souls in heaven, not bodies, but they can appear to their living relatives in whatever way they wish. Sometimes they visit as babies and sometimes they appear to grow up in respect of the years that have passed since their departing.

Where do people live in the afterlife, do they have houses like they would have had on earth? Is it a mirror image of our earth where they can be who they want and do what they want?
In the realms closest to the earth you can 'create', or have created for you, a home which reflects something you might have had on earth, but in the higher realms you no longer have the need to live in a home – you just 'are'.

What about those who have done wrong in this life, do they get a second chance in the afterlife?
. . . and a third, and a fourth. If you want to learn from mistakes then this is the goal – it's all part of our learning experience. There is no wrong or right as we understand it exactly, it's all just practice.

Will I meet my baby that I miscarried, and will my parents see the grandchild they have never met?
Absolutely!

And can those who die in old age appear to us as a younger person?
They choose how they appear to us, yes.

I took the heartbreaking decision of terminating my baby at twenty-two weeks of pregnancy in August,

as my baby had severe problems and no chance of survival. I would like to know more about what happens to babies like mine – will they know about us? I would also like to know if my baby would forgive me. I've been trying to find a book on this but can't find anything.

There is quite a lot of information about this subject but it's spread around in many different books and so it's hard to find. I will explain the conclusion I have come to after reading hundreds of books on near-death experiences, deep hypnotic trance and dream-visitation experiences. As you read more and more of these and realize none really contradict each other, this information becomes 'fact' to me. My advice is to take this if it feels right to you and ignore it as you feel fit. I appreciate it's a controversial subject.

When a baby is terminated (the soul), it already knows in advance that there is a high chance of this happening. Souls pick lives for many reasons and often when a soul passes over early in life it's because it is trying out a body for the first time (and may have picked a short life for that reason), or it's part of a pre-agreed contract between them and us (the baby soul and the parent) . . . I appreciate this is of little comfort to the bereaved and there really isn't enough space to do this subject justice here. Books by Dolores Cannon and Dr Michael Newton (in particular Newton's *Journey of Souls* and *Destiny of Souls*) may explain the life contracts we make in more detail.

There is nothing to forgive. Be at peace knowing we make the best choices we can at the time. It is often impossible to go back and recall how we felt and recreate in our mind what the situation was at the time. Sometimes there is no right or wrong choice – we just have to make *a* choice, and live with it – and that is the hard part!

I must note here that if souls are meant to be with our family (or soul groups) then they will come back in the next appropriate body within the group. Souls can reincarnate as the children or grandchildren, cousins or friends of the family, for example. There are many stories of young children remembering their previous life with the family – strange, I know! So if the soul is part of your group, you'll see them again (and again and again).

When you're in heaven with your loved ones, do you stay together or do you at one point separate again? I have in mind my husband, who passed away two years ago.
Well, that would depend. We do incarnate with the same people over and over again and if your husband was part of your immediate soul group then you will spend time together on the other side too. You'll be learning together and can socialize and so on. Even if he wasn't and you want to spend time together then you can . . . or not!

If we live many lives, then what happens if our loved ones are reincarnated into another life when they die? Does this mean they are no longer around us, as they are now a different living person?
When we enter a body we bring part of the soul energy with us . . . Imagine the soul is a glass of water and you

pour half into one glass and drink the other half. It's still the same glass of water but it's just in two different places. Some of the energy essence always remains behind on the heaven-side so even if the soul has reincarnated they will still be there to greet you.

That does mean, though, that there is now less of the soul in heaven and it makes it much more difficult to communicate with those on the earth-side. Let me give you a strange example from my own experience.

Sorry I Can't Visit Any More!

After my grandmother passed over she was a regular visitor from the other side and often appeared in dreams; not just to me – she visited many of the family from the afterlife. One day my daughter (maybe aged around ten, I forget) had been playing with her sister and her cousins when she broke off from the group, walked over to me and her aunts and randomly said, 'Great Granny wants to say goodbye, she's going to be born into a new body and won't be able to visit any more.' Then she just walked back to the rest of the children and carried on playing.

My sisters and I all sat there open-mouthed. It just seemed such a bizarre thing for her to have said. Later on when we were alone I asked her about it again and this time she had no memory of having even made the comment in the first place! Had my grandmother reached out to her great-granddaughter to communicate? I have to say *yes* because after that she never appeared again!

I know that her soul will be there to greet me when I pass over but, with the soul split, she is no longer able to contact me here on this side of life. I hope that helps explain your question a little more.

Do they always hear us when we talk to them no matter what time of day or night?
Time has no meaning in heaven. 'Time' is an earth concept, a way we organize our life. Outside of the earth everything is happening now, so I see no reason why time should be a deciding factor.

My dad is a regular visitor and when I ask for him to come he doesn't always appear right away ... it's as if someone (my own spirit guide or guardian angel?) gives and fetches him. If you want your deceased loved ones to hear your thoughts or words, it seems to work best when you think of them for a while ... maybe looking at a loving photograph or holding a possession that belonged to them. If they are close you will certainly get the sensation of this, if my postbag of readers' experiences is anything to go by anyway!

How do they decide who comes to collect you when you pass over to the other side.
'They' don't decide really, it's more about who was important to us in life. My dad appeared in a dream to myself and one of my sisters where we saw queues of people waiting

to greet him on his return to heaven. We were privileged to glimpse his 'welcome home' party. This group included (at the front) his mum, dad and brother, followed by his aunts (who helped to bring him up). Then behind that were other relatives, close friends and even work colleagues and old neighbours (he was clearly a popular man). There were many souls in the dream that I did not recognize, and my sister said the same. I was also aware of many dogs!

Do they do the same things there as they did on earth, like drinking, going to bingo, smoking and have birthdays and Christmas?
Well, they can, but these are part of our earthly thoughts and feelings about life, so in time these earthly needs are shed away. Bingo seems fairly unimportant when you are a soul who can fly!

Do the people I love wait to see me when it is my time to pass over, or will some of them be reincarnated?
Some will have reincarnated (see earlier question), but you will still be able to see them as part of their essence remains heaven-side. Important people in your soul group will likely wait for you so that you can incarnate again as a group when you are all ready.

If they are reincarnated, does that mean I will never see them again as I know them?
When you first see them on the other side (when you yourself pass on) you will recognize them as you knew

them. But you will also remember them as they look in their spirit bodies or spirit selves and will feel perfectly comfortable with that too.

What happens to the really bad and evil people when they die? Do they exist with all the rest of the spirits?
Not at first, no. They will be drawn to others of a similar vibration (state of learning). They will be given all assistance to atone for what they have done; and given the opportunity of seeing, feeling and experiencing the results of their choices. They may need much time to learn from this.

Do we still do housework in heaven and have TV?
Would you want a TV in heaven? I'm sure you wouldn't! No, there is no housework, there is no dust! People describe everything as clean and beautiful.

I read once that before we come to earth we already know how we will leave and we have agreed to this beforehand. It was also said that we chose our parents.
That's true and there are thousands of case histories of people who recall all of this information (many of these stories from hypnosis sessions where clients are put into the very deepest of trance states). We pick our parents, families and friends because they can most help us to learn the lessons we need to learn. Naturally, they

form part of our soul group. Although you might not always thank them, they are playing their roles as we are playing ours.

When we die do we get the chance to put right the bad choices we made in life? And if we do, will we come back as a better, wiser person because we have learnt from our past wrongdoings?
Yes, that is the theory. Some people whizz through their lifetimes really quickly and others of us come back again and again until we get it right! Some little things take many lifetimes to integrate. If you overeat, overspend or are always rude to your parents, you bet you're coming back to get that right!

Because we live such long lives now compared to hundreds of years ago it can often seem that we live several lives in one go. We change careers and partners, live in different types of homes and interact with many different people.

We also make the same mistakes over and over. For example:

- We diet, lose weight and then diet again – maybe one lesson is to eat with care?
- We overspend our money, save and then spend too much again – is money a lesson for you?
- You find you go from one abusive relationship to another – do you need to learn self-esteem?

You get the idea!

When someone passes away, do they come and say goodbye?

Not always, but this is a growing phenomenon and people all around the world are having this type of experience right now. Sometimes the spirit says goodbye when the person is unaware that their friend or relative has even passed on. Of course, this adds even more proof that the encounter is a real one. So they visit you in a dream-visitation experience to say goodbye, then a friend telephones the next morning to tell you that the person has died. Of course it's real!

Do we still have to go to work in heaven? Or do we work for a higher being, doing other kinds of work like angels do?

We don't have to do anything if we don't want to and some souls will take many years to relax and explore. There comes a point though where souls are ready to learn or teach. We are not assigned roles usually; we may choose to do things which give us joy. In some visits from the other side, souls will tell their grieving relatives what they are up to in heaven so we have a great deal of understanding of the types of things they can do.

Are all our family and friends together along with our pets?

Together or close by usually. They may also have joint pursuits and separate ones. Pets have their own areas in heaven but we can choose to be with them if and when we wish.

I have moved from the family home since my parents passed away. Do they know where I am now to keep an eye on me? I hope so, Jacky.

Where you live will make no difference at all. They are drawn to our soul energy rather than our living accommodation. People have experienced visits from the deceased when they were staying in friends' homes, on holiday abroad and even when flying in an aeroplane!

Do we interact with only certain people in heaven or could we hang out with Elvis if we wanted to?

What a fun question! As before, we are drawn to be with people who are similar to our vibration but souls have explained how they have seen famous people during near-death experiences and several people have written to me to share stories of visits from 'famous' souls (the souls of well-known people on earth). I think these souls are aware of our connection to them and so this in itself may draw a visit . . . if you're really lucky.

I once had a visit from the soul of the late Princess Margaret but I asked the spirit to go away because I thought it couldn't be her. Then I discovered the next day that she had passed away so perhaps it was her after all.

I also once had a dream-visitation experience from the late Michael Jackson. It was months after he had passed away. In my dream I was at the front of a huge queue of people; there were thousands waiting behind me. Security were standing at the front of the queue and I was let into what looked like the foyer of a grand hotel. The walls and floor were made of a type of marble and standing at the front, looking much as he did in life, was the late Michael Jackson.

I recall feeling overwhelmed at the privilege of meeting him in this way and as I did so I understood that many thousands had been ahead of me in the queue. Michael held out his arms to me and held me tightly. In that instant I felt his soul and even though controversy followed him in life, his soul was like an ice-diamond, full of light and totally pure. His mission on earth had been to share unconditional love, especially with children. Then as soon as it had begun, it was over and I woke up. Was it real? I can only tell you that it followed the rules of all the other afterlife-contact experiences I've ever had and it has remained as clear to me today as it did on the day it happened.

I've had two other people who have shared their own spirit contact from Michael (dream visits which occurred to them in a very similar way to the experience I'd had myself). I've also had two letters from people who had dream visits from the Australian animal man Steve Irwin, who passed away in 2006. One lady explained that she hadn't been a massive fan of him in life but felt extreme sympathy towards his family and great sadness when he passed. Maybe this was enough to draw him to her? As with my own experience, it was many months after he passed on that she had her experience, almost as if, like me, she was further back along the queue!

Do people stay the age they are when they pass over? If they had any medical/physical problems in life, do they have them in the afterlife?
With healing, in time the soul no longer carries these. However, some people come into their current life with scars from their passing in their last life! This is the explanation that the soul comes up with when the person is put under deep hypnotic trance. Maybe, like me, that strange birthmark and circle of moles of the same size are the result of a past life where I was killed by a bow and arrow . . . Something to think about, anyway. But that is a whole other book! And as we've mentioned earlier, souls can appear to us in whatever way they wish.

My father was cremated after he passed away rather than buried. Will it affect his ability to communicate with the family?
Not at all, it's the soul that communicates, not the body.

Conclusion

'Death is the golden key that opens the
palace of eternity.'

John Milton

Heaven

Let's review the evidence once more.

Millions – billions – of people, both now and in the
past, believe that heaven is a real place; that life continues
after physical death. Cultures all around the world think
that once their physical body dies, their soul will ascend to
a higher place. That place has been called Dreamtime,
Nirvana, paradise and heaven, amongst many other names.
Is it possible that all these people are wrong? Yes, it's possible, but it's improbable.

At one point we had only our faith to guide us; we
wanted to believe that heaven was a real place and our
teachings, family beliefs and cultural background may
have suggested that it was true. These days we have so
much more information to guide us.

- The near-death experience (something that
  billions have been through over the years) gives

239

many a glimpse into the other realms. People come back after visiting the other side of life.

- The deceased continue to visit their loved ones, us human bodies, here on the earth-side of life. Spirits pop over for a visit . . . they must go back somewhere when they've done, right?
- Some have found themselves drawn up to the higher realms during daydream states, meditation, when they are unconscious or sleeping.
- Psychic mediums bring messages back from the other side.
- People in deep hypnotic trance states will recall quite naturally their pre-birth home in heaven.

So many have seen heaven and then come back to tell us all about it afterwards.

What is it Like?

You've read story after story which describes heaven. I bet you were as surprised as I was to learn that so many of their descriptions seem to be of the place. We've been told that heaven is a place full of love; that it has lots of wonderful green open spaces and beautiful buildings . . . and that colours exist in heaven that the viewer didn't recognize from life in their earthly bodies; colours our souls can see but the eyes of the limited human body cannot.

Some have met angels, deceased loved ones and pets they owned on earth. These beings appear to comfort and reassure them whilst the visitors are temporarily in the heavenly space. Sometimes they are lucky enough to be shown around a little but always they are sent back into their bodies because it was not 'their time'.

We've seen border crossings of many descriptions. A heavenly gate, stairway or river crossing seems to mark the way between our side of life and theirs. I have no doubt that when our time comes we'll be welcomed back to the place which many who've witnessed describe as our 'real home'.

People have described their visits to me, saying, 'I know my body was asleep but I was completely awake and aware.' They tell me, 'I can't explain it but I know it was true.' They are stunned themselves when they share their experiences, telling me, 'It was amazing . . . it changed my life . . . I felt comforted and could move on with my life.'

Some readers have told me how their deceased loved ones share information which has yet to occur in their lives. It's as if, in heaven, the spirits can see ahead slightly, and are aware of our future life. This shows very much how time does not exist in the way that we understand it here on earth.

Some have received extraordinary signs, which vary from the simple feather experience to more dramatic encounters with the afterlife. Each has something personal happen to them . . . it means something to us. We know and understand that the phenomenon is a message from a deceased love one.

We've also looked at some extraordinary stories of 'life' not existing in the way that we assume it does. You've read about time slips, past lives and classrooms in heaven. Sometimes I know that it's difficult to keep your mind open to ideas that appear far-fetched and bizarre. To keep an open mind means that you are stretched and bent like a pretzel! I know . . . I know . . . it's hard!

If you are new to this phenomenon I appreciate how much harder this has been for you. Readers of my other works may be more ready for some of this 'spooky stuff', but don't give up yet! I hope that it has expanded your world a little and that, when you are ready, you decide to pick up where you left off and do some more investigating of your own. You decide for yourself what is real to you.

I first started looking at life after death thirty-five years ago when my mother picked up the book *Life After Life* by Dr Raymond Moody; a book about the near-death phenomenon. I was hooked and have been reading every book and account I have been able to get my hands on since. Now that's a long time and a lot of books! I can tell you that in more recent years I have concentrated my efforts into writing books about the afterlife, not just reading them. I'll give you a reading list at the back of this book so that you can find some of my other work if you are interested, but don't forget your e-reader and your local library as a source of further information too.

If you want to reach me to talk about what happened to you then I welcome your interaction. I love to hear stories of your own experiences and you can reach me at my website (where I also have pages of more free information).

After so much research I am completely convinced that the soul continues as a living personality-energy after physical death. Death of the physical body is NOT the end of life. Our loved ones continue in their new life in heaven and one day – when it's our time – we will too. Heaven, dear reader, is real!

Thanks for reading . . . keep in touch!

Jacky x

Further Reading and More Information

Other Books by Jacky Newcomb

An Angel Treasury (Harper Element, 2004)
A Little Angel Love (Harper Element, 2005)
An Angel Saved My Life (Harper Element, 2006)
An Angel By My Side (Harper Element, 2006)
An Angel Held My Hand (Harper Element, 2007)
Angels Watching Over Me (Hay House, 2007; reprinted 2009)
A Faerie Treasury, co-written with Alicen Geddes-Ward (Hay House, 2007)
Angel Kids (Hay House, 2008)
Dear Angel Lady (Hay House, 2009)
I Can See Angels (Hay House, 2010)
Angel Secrets (Octopus, 2010)
Healed By an Angel (Hay House, 2011)
Call Me When You Get to Heaven, co-written with Madeline Richardson (Piatkus, 2011)
Protected By Angels (Hay House, 2012)
Angel Blessings (Octopus, 2013)

Other Products by Jacky Newcomb

Angel Secrets Divination Cards (Octopus)
Angels DVD (New World Music)
Healing With Your Guardian Angel CD (Paradise Music)
Meet Your Guardian Angel CD (Paradise Music)
Angel Workshop CD (Paradise Music)
Ghost Workshop CD (Paradise Music)

Further Reading

The Birth Called Death, Kathie Jordan (White Cloud
   Press, 2003)
Journey of Souls, Dr Michael Newton (Llewellyn
   Publications, 1994)
Between Death and Life, Dolores Cannon
   (Gateway, 2003)
http://www.near-death.com
http://www.victorzammit.com

Other Online Information

You can find Jacky Newcomb on her social networking sites:

Jacky's Twitter feed: twitter.com/JackyNewcomb

Jacky's personal Facebook page:
https://www.facebook.com/pages/Jacky-Newcomb/
117853386746

Jacky's Angel Facebook page:
http's://www.facebook.com/AngelsByJackyNewcomb

Jacky's personal website:
Jacky Newcomb.com

Other Contact Information

Jacky welcomes contact from fans. You can reach her via the form at her website, through her social media sites at Twitter and Facebook (preferred) or via the publisher at the following address. If you would like a personal reply or autographed card, please include a large stamped addressed envelope:

Jacky Newcomb (author)
c/o Penguin Books Ltd,
80 Strand,
London
WC2R ORL